The Origins Of Western Civilization

The Origins of Western Civilization:

A Survey of the Economic, Social and Political Forces That Have Revolutionized the Western World

By Dr. Harry Elmer Barnes

ISBN: 0-9742303-8-3 ISBN: 978-0-9742303-8-2

Published by:

THE FOUNDATION FOR ECONOMIC LIBERTY
THE BARNES REVIEW
P.O. Box 15877
Washington, D.C. 20003

1-877-773-9077 toll free
www.barnesreview.com

A subscription to THE BARNES REVIEW historical magazine is $46 for one year (six issues) and $78 for two years (12 issues) inside the U.S. Outside the U.S: Canada/Mexico: $65 per year. All other nations: $80 per year sent via air mail. Send payment with request to TBR, P.O. Box 15877, Washington, D.C. 20003. Call 1-877-773-9077 toll free to charge to Visa or MasterCard. Order online at www.barnesreview.com.

The Origins Of Western Civilization

A Survey of the Economic,
Social and Political Forces
That Have Revolutionized
The Western World

BY HARRY ELMER BARNES, PH.D.

An oil painting of Harry Elmer Barnes created by Virginia True.

TABLE OF CONTENTS

The Compleat Historian: The First American Revisionist

HARRY ELMER BARNES was indisputably one of the great intellects of his, or any, era. Historian, sociologist, criminologist and social reformer—mentor to scholars worldwide—Professor Barnes wrote more than 40 books, including a variety of college textbooks which were standards in their respective fields. Historian Murray Rothbard described Barnes as "The Compleat Historian."

Born in Auburn, New York on June 15, 1889, Barnes received his doctorate from Columbia University and pursued post-graduate studies at Harvard. He taught history and historical sociology at prestigious universities throughout the country.

His two-volume *The History of Western Civilization* (1935) and *An Intellectual and Cultural History of the Western World* (1937) remain timeless classics.

The Genesis of the World War (1926), *In Quest of Truth and Justice* (1928) and *World Politics in Modern Civilization* (1930) were major contributions by Barnes to a full and accurate understanding of the events that led to the First World War.

While Barnes' post-war studies were highly controversial, his subsequent scholarly inquiries into the causes of the Second World War were even more so. *Perpetual War for Perpetual Peace* (1953), edited by Barnes, explored the forces that led to the world wars of the 20th century.

"Truth," said Barnes, "is always the first war casualty. The emotional disturbances and distortions in historical writing are greatest in wartime." Barnes' aim was "to correct the historical record in the light of a more complete collection of historical facts, a more calm political atmosphere, and a more objective attitude."

Barnes died in 1968. He is remembered by the sobriquet given him by historian Carl Becker: "The Learned Crusader." THE BARNES REVIEW strives to carry on Barnes' passionate dedication to bringing history into accord with the facts.

The Remarkable
Harry Elmer Barnes

D uring his amazing career, Harry Elmer Barnes wrote hundreds of books and pamphlets and thousands of letters. Although his primary reputation is as an historian—the founder of WWI and WWII revisionism—he is also known as a sociologist and friend and tutor to other scholars and writers, such as David Hoggan, the author of the magnum opus on the origins of WWII, *The Forced War—When Peaceful Revision Failed*.

Yet Barnes' political position cannot be fitted into any niche. Consistency—according to our orthodox standards—is no hallmark of his career, yet no one could have been more consistent in championing peace and the rights of the underdog, liberalism in thinking but firmness—even harness and dogmatism—when it came to the re-examination of questions deemed settled by propagandists and orthodox historians.

Throughout his career, Barnes at one time or another fell out with each of his friends over interpretations of events, but always only temporarily because they all knew him for the kind, generous, and loyal friend that he was.

Barnes was anything but an armchair philosopher; he loved to hike, hunt and fish with his friends.

As a humanitarian, Barnes recognized that war was a curse upon humans yet he also knew that war is the greatest shaper of history, an essential part of it, for better or worse. He accepted that, although hating war as a killer of millions, hoping that someday, perhaps, war itself could be vanquished.

Thus, he supported international efforts to avoid war even though he was not sanguine about their chances for success.

Top: Barnes with Revisionist Group, Berlin, 1927. Barnes is in the front row. Alfred von Wegerer and Baron Rosen are to Barnes' left. **Middle row**: At left, Barnes, an avid sportsman and gun collector, is shown with a mule dear he bagged in Diamond Valley in 1948. At right, Barnes tips his hat to Willis and Elisabeth Carto as he comes up a hill on his Malibu ranch after searching for a Bird of Paradise plant. **Bottom:** Barnes and wife Jean on a lecture trip to Spokane, Wash. in 1940.

It was Barnes' passionate commitment to truth that jeopardized the applause of scholars and supporters during the last 20 years of his life. Because of America's intervention into what then became the second world war, the interventionists saw him as an obstacle to their murderous plans. He lost his repute as a scholar and leader but still he refused to be stampeded by the war hysteria led by FDR, the major spokesman and organizer for war.

American intervention into the European war of 1914 made it a "world" war. After the Allies won, Barnes objected to the one-sided claims by the intellectual armchair warriors that the war guilt was Germany's alone. He realized that such claims were merely a carry-over of the mendacious pro-war propaganda of the practical men who profit from blood. He knew that before war, and especially during it, ingenious mythmakers are paid by governments and war profiteers to dream up lies calculated to get taxpayers in the mood to pay, and young men in the army to get killed. So he and a few other honest historians and writers did their best to "revise" the history written by the propagandists. Thus they became "revisionists."

The main task after WWI, as well as after WWII, was to discredit the war guilt theory—the sophomoric idea that only Germany and the other Central Powers were guilty of starting the wars; that peace-loving England, France and the United States were set upon by Germany and Austria, and again by Japan in 1941, and that the angelic politicians of the Allies had no choice but to fight back.

Fortunately, Barnes lived long enough after 1945 to see the one-sided tide begin to turn among historians and a movement emerged to question all of America's imperialist wars. Composed of all political persuasions, they were united only by what Barnes cherished more than anything else—truth and the courage to speak it.

As you read this small yet ambitious volume, you will encounter the reflections and conclusions about Western history, where we have been and where, as a civilization, we are bound—the conclusions of the remarkable American scholar, Harry Elmer Barnes.

—Willis A. Carto
August 2008

Detail of face of Emperor Justinian from the mosaic of Justinian and Retinue at the apse entry, San Vitale, Ravenna, circa A.D. 546.

The Modern Man

The modern man who is able, through the aid of the recently provided mechanisms for the communication and dissemination of information, to familiarize himself with the more important events which have taken place throughout the world in the previous 24 hours, finds it very difficult to comprehend that during the greater part of recorded history the chief successive centers of civilization have occupied an extremely limited area of settlement. Additionally, their inhabitants have had only the most imperfect and tardy knowledge of what was contemporaneously taking place even within this small area. Oriental history developed and passed chiefly within the confines of what Professor J.H. Breasted has called the "fertile crescent" of the valleys of the Nile, Tigris and Euphrates. Classical history added to this area of historic activity the coast of the Mediterranean Sea, with a varying depth of hinterland.

Medieval civilization, driven on primarily by the expansive power of Christianity, working on the basis of the ruins of the Roman imperial system, brought within the realm of chronicled human endeavor northern and western Europe. While one should not forget the flourishing north European civilization of prehistoric or proto-historic times, which has been revealed by Joseph Dechelette, Oscar Montelius, Preston Peet, Neil Munro, and others, or the advanced and extremely old civilizations of India and China, it is fairly accurate to maintain that until the opening of the 16th century most of the great historic civilizations had arisen and had declined, all of them, within an area not greater than that of the present United States of America. The subsequent history of the world in its larger aspects has been a process, based upon exploration, colonization, and mechanical invention, which has involved: (1) extending the area of historical interaction between peoples; (2) breaking down the earlier localism, isolation, provincialism and stability; and (3) utilizing the reactions of these changes upon the original European centers of worldwide expansion.

Crusaders and Saracens battle outside of a Christian stronghold in the Holy Land.

CHAPTER ONE

The Dynamic Forces
Behind the Expansion
Of European Civilization

O f all the forces producing the general process of European expansion in modern times, the oldest and most enduring, if not the most important, has been the missionary impulse of Christianity. This not only widened the area of European civilization during the period from the fall of the Roman Empire to the height of the Middle Ages, but ever since that time has maintained its energy and activity. As professors James Harvey Robinson and Charles Beard have well expressed the matter:"The way for imperialism has been smoothed by the missionaries. There have always been ardent Christians ready to obey the command,'Go ye into all the world and preach the gospel to every creature.' No sooner was a new country brought to the attention of Europeans than missionaries flocked thither with traders and soldiers."

The Crusades (1095-1291) constitute the first notable religious movement which possesses great significance for the subsequent expansion of Europe. While the intellectual and economic results of the Crusades, centering in the appropriation of Muslim culture and the development of trading relations between East and West by Italian city-states, were much more significant for posterity than the temporary triumph of the Cross over the Crescent, it is certain that, without the initial religious impulse, there would have been no possibility for the development of the subsequent significant intellectual and economic interaction between Europe and the East which followed the Crusades. In the period of European exploration which ushered in the Commercial Revolution, the Catholic missionaries—Franciscans and Dominicans, and later the Jesuits—were in the vanguard of expansion. About the beginning of the 19th century the Protestant missions entered into the campaign of conversion overseas, which has since been in the process of ever greater expansion and more perfect organization. Profoundly moved by the semi-fanatical conviction of the uniqueness and the superiority of Christianity over all other forms of world religions, these missionaries have often rudely violated the theology and the "morés" of the native non-Western peoples. This has frequently been followed by the persecution or the extermination of the missionaries, which has in turn opened the way for the military intervention of modern governments, driven on by eager capitalists anxiously awaiting the opportunity for investment in these underdeveloped areas. As Dr. Lawrence Dennis, Mr. MacDonald, Prof. Kenneth Scott Latourette, and Prof. E.C. Moore have shown, the missionary movement has always been closely linked up with the expansion of European civilization and the growth of modern imperialism.

One of the most persistent and effective of all influences stimulating the process of expansion has been the desire to develop more extensive and profitable trading relations. It was the trade which the Italian merchants, carrying the Crusaders to the East, built up with the Levant that produced the flourishing Mediterranean commercial activity which was both a harbinger and a cause of the later overseas exploration. The jealousy on the part of the western or seaboard European powers regarding the Italian monopoly of the trade with the East led to attempts, first made by the Portuguese, to discover another route to the Indies. This resulted in that great era of exploration which brought about the Commercial Revolution and the beginnings of modern world trade. From 1550 to the present day the development of world trade has been one of the most notable dynamic agencies promoting the expansion movement, particularly since it has been reinforced by the Industrial Revolution. At the present time, in conjunction with the search for raw materials, it quite overshadows all other stimuli in this field.

A powerful psychological and political motive for expansion is to be seen in modern nationalism, a force which has been developing with ever greater intensity since the first appearance of the dynastic national states during the 16th and 17th centuries. It was nationalism that promoted the narrow and exclusive economic and political policy, known as "Mercantilism," which dominated European commercial and colonial methods from the close of the 16th century until its overthrow by the economic liberals following the middle of the 18th century. It was nationalism which combined with trade rivalry to produce the series of European wars over colonial interests in the late 17th and 18th centuries. In the period of recent national imperialism since 1870 the nationalistic or patriotic impulse has played a most important part. Territory overseas has been sought as compensation for European losses, as in the case of France; for the purpose of stimulating national pride, as was most evident in the case of Germany; or as a means of providing investment opportunities for national capital, which has been the case with all modern nations, but most particularly true of Great Britain, the United States and Germany. In the last half century, the period in which the capitalistic class gradually displaced the landlords and became the dominant group in the control of modern governments, patriotic pride in national expansion overseas has been assiduously fostered by the governing classes in order to gain psychological support for their commercial and imperialistic policies.

Another set of influences promoting European expansion was highly varied and complex, but may be described vaguely, if accurately, as psychological. There was, of course, plenty of psychological motivation in the desire to save the heathen, to secure markets, and to advance national power and prestige, but there were powerful incentives over and beyond these.

There was offered the opportunity for adventure and the possibility of achieving wealth and glory. Curiosity was an important factor inducing many a mariner, explorer and settler to venture forth from his European home. Resentment over oppression—religious, political, or economic—stimulated many to seek their fortunes abroad. The general atmosphere of the age of expansion was one to catch the imagination of the daring and roving spirits of that era, and many succumbed who were not forced by circumstances to better their lot in the new lands.

All of the motives leading to overseas expansion were powerfully advanced and given new energy by the Industrial Revolution of the 18th and 19th centuries, which furnished the perfected mechanism of modern expansion and augmented the economic motives for imperialistic activity. The vast increase in the productivity of marketable commodities through the application of the machine processes and the factory system has led to the search for more markets. The improved methods of oceanic transportation and of the communication of information have made the search for world markets more feasible and successful. Explorations in the underdeveloped regions have revealed the wealth of raw materials to be obtained from these districts, and the increase of available capital has led to a desire to develop the economic potentialities of these backward regions. This has been made easy through the fact that the industrial and scientific revolutions affected the military as well as the economic field and provided the modern technique of war which puts the natives completely at the mercy of the European invaders. Modern imperialism has been an historic complex of ever greater significance, which draws its motive power from the realms of religious fanaticism, commercial ambitions, national prides and the multifarious impulses coming from modern capitalism.

The motives of European expansion may be summarized admirably in Professor Norman Shepherd's epigrammatic statement that those who left Europe for experience overseas were driven primarily by the desire to spread the Gospel, to accumulate gold and to cover themselves and their country with glory. "Gospel, gold and glory" was the slogan, conscious or unconscious, of the rise of the new order.

"War is the most striking instance of the failure of intelligence to master the problem of human relationships."

—Harry Elmer Barnes

A copy of Gutenberg's Bible is created using a printing press. The printing press—more than any single invention—may have influenced the course of world history.

CHAPTER TWO

Overseas Expansion
And the Origins of
Modern Times:
The Basis of Western History

The present tendency is to lay much less stress than formerly upon such cataclysmic events as the fall of Constantinople in 1453 and the artistic and religious movements popularly termed the Renaissance and the Reformation. Constantinople suffered a long decline before the Ottoman Turks finally captured it. Its eclipse was due to slow but very great changes in European economic organization that curtailed its monopoly of markets, and to certain military movements in Asia affecting its sources of supplies. The Renaissance, or intellectual awakening of the 14th and 15th centuries, is now generally regarded as a mere acceleration of a movement already well under way, and having its roots far back in the Middle Ages. Its intellectual, scientific, and economic atmosphere was derived at least as much from the contemporary European situation as from the classical revival which has given the period its name. There is no divorcing it, as a factor in modern history, from the material facts which underlay and surround it.

Chief among these are the material facts which underlay cities, the invention of printing, and the great expansion of European economic contacts that began with the Crusades, merged in the overseas explorations and colonizing projects, and is still going on as the exploitation of backward regions of the Earth.

Neither the Renaissance nor the Reformation or Protestant revolt was in any true sense a "cause" of the great changes in European life which followed. Both were dramatic but incidental factors in a general situation. Historians of the Reformation are interesting themselves more and more in such economic matters as the effects of the rapid development of trade and industry upon peasant life, politics and the point of view of Europeans generally. It is impossible to consider the revolt from the church separately from the flood of printed books and pamphlets which would not have been possible without the inventions of the preceding century, or to peruse the pamphlets themselves without perceiving the fundamental driving force of the economic issues they raised. The bourgeoisie, or enterprising middle class, and the national state had acquired a potential force that was bound to assert itself before very long. Whenever this should take place, the overturn of the medieval system was inevitable through the play of forces which it had itself produced. From the Crusades to the present, the most impressive and constant factor in the changes that have appeared is the expansion of trade. During the Middle Ages, this exerted itself chiefly on inland seas, rivers and caravan routes. In early modern times, before the age of railways, the overseas phase was the most striking.

"Historians of the Reformation are interesting themselves more and morein such economic matters as the effects of the rapid development of trade and industry upon peasant life, politics and the point of view of Europeans generally."

Illustration of Vasco da Gama as found in *Oceanos*, Numero 33, page 59.

CHAPTER THREE

The Background of the Commercial Revolution

W hile the volume of European trade during the so-called Dark Ages was greater than was once supposed, it is true that the earliest notable development of medieval trade followed the Crusades. The peoples of western Europe desired the spices from the Malay Archipelago and the East Indies to make their coarse and ill-preserved food palatable. They further wished to secure precious stones from Persia and India; drugs, perfumes, gums, dyes and woods from the Indies, China and Japan; and draperies, cloth, rugs and fine steel work from Persia and Asia Minor. The desire for these commodities was awakened by the contact with the East during the Crusades and was exploited by the Italian city-states. Their merchants purchased these products which had been brought from the East through the Red Sea, Asia Minor or Turkestan, took them back to Europe and sold them to distributing merchants.

It was long a venerable tradition in European history that the occupation of the above-mentioned eastern trade-routes by the Turks following 1453 constituted the chief cause of the downfall of the Italian city-states and the reason for the subsequent development of attempts to discover new routes to the East. Professor A.H. Lybyer has shown, however, that Thorold Rogers' and M. D'Avenel's statistics of prices following 1453 indicate no appreciable effect of Turkish occupation on the volume or prices of commodities coming from the East to Europe, and he also calls attention to the fact that the Turks did not occupy the southern routes until nearly a generation after overseas communication had been established with the Indies. Rather, it seems that the chief cause of overseas exploration was the jealousy of the developing western European seaboard powers and merchants in regard to the Italian monopoly of the Eastern trade. With the Portuguese and Spanish the religious motive was also very powerful. The Portuguese, under Henry the Navigator and Bartholomew Diaz, began in the middle of the 15th century the explorations that ended in the successful voyage of Vasco da Gama to India in 1492. Under Spanish auspices Columbus discovered America in 1492, and Magellan's fleet circumnavigated the globe in 1519-22. These and subsequent explorations opened the way for further expansion and constituted the geographical foundation of the Commercial Revolution and the dawn of modern history.

*"The first war casualty
is the truth."*

—Harry Elmer Barnes

Spanish conqueror of Mexico Hernando Cortez (1485-1547), entering Tlascala with his army after the victory of Otumba, circa 1530.

CHAPTER FOUR

The Rival Commercial Empires

The epoch from 1500 to 1763 in world politics may be most intelligently viewed as the era of the rise and struggles of what have been called the "rival commercial empires." This period started with the rise of the Portuguese to commercial supremacy following the return of Vasco da Gama from India in 1499, and ended with the defeat of the French in North America and India by Great Britain in 1763.

Taking advantage of her priority in explorations in this region, Portugal occupied the Spice Islands and points along the Indian and African coasts, and built up a considerable trade. Her internal strength was not equal, however, to the strain imposed by this over-extensive and rapid external expansion. She lacked the naval power to defend her trading monopoly; she was unable to organize a systemic and competent distribution service for the Eastern commodities; she had few commodities to be taken east in exchange for materials purchased; and a corrupt officialdom made it impossible for her to control unscrupulous traders. Her decline invited foreign aggression, and in 1560 Portugal was annexed to Spain and held in subjugation for some 60 years.

Spain vied with Portugal as an early contender for colonial and commercial supremacy, occupying the greater part of the New World, especially South and Central America, and several groups of Pacific islands. The great wealth thereby secured and controlled by Spain might have made that country the greatest of modern powers, had it been guided by a wise administrative and fiscal policy, but such wisdom was lacking and the Spanish decline was only slightly less rapid and complete than that of Portugal. The excessively strict regulation of the colonial trade crippled commerce with the mother country and invited smuggling; a cruel and wasteful system of native labor lessened productivity in the colonies; the expulsion of Jews and Moors from Spain drove her monied classes beyond her borders, while repudiation of debts forced withdrawal of German credit; religious bigotry and fiscal exaction lost the rich provinces of the Netherlands; the Inquisition crushed out all intellectual originality and initiative; and the loss of the Armada in 1588 meant the end of Spanish naval supremacy. At the beginning of the 17th century Spain was becoming that second-rate power which she has since remained.

Stirred to action by Spanish oppression, the Netherlands enjoyed the commercial supremacy of Europe for more than a half-century following 1590, occupying most of the old Portuguese possessions in the East, as well as valuable areas in North and South America. But the Dutch were not equal to the task of building up a permanent commercial empire of great extent. Like ancient Athens, the Netherlands was a loosely united group of jealous city-states rather than a compact national unit; the "Spanish Fury" helped to ruin Antwerp, and the closing of the Scheldt ended its prosperity; the Dutch devoted their energy chiefly to commercial activity with little attention to permanent colonial policy; and in the contest with England under Cromwell and during the early years of the Restoration the Dutch were thoroughly worsted. Though Dutch naval and colonial power was shattered in the middle of the 17th century, the Netherlands retained its primary importance in the trade of the world well into the 18th century.

France was prevented from making an early entry into the commercial and colonial scramble by the religious diversions that led to the civil wars of the latter part of the 16th century. Even when she did make some systematic attempt to contend as a first-class commercial and colonizing power, her strength was sapped by the suicidal policy of Louis XIV, who, at the critical moment, wasted the national energy of France in futile attempts to extend the eastern boundary of that country. France was immensely more rich and powerful than England in the 17th and 18th centuries, but lost out in the final conflict because of a corrupt administration, the failure to devote her resources to the strengthening of her colonies, and the adoption of a fatally weak colonial policy—that of scattered military occupation. Though England had, by 1763, become the leading colonial and commercial state of Europe, she was until the time of Elizabeth a relatively small and weak state. The rising British sea-power was based upon the naval training afforded her sailors by buccaneering expeditions against the Spaniards and was proved by the destruction of the Spanish Armada in 1588. The Dutch were vanquished in the middle of the 17th century and a duel of a 100 years with France for colonial supremacy began. Aside from the fact that England took her colonial enterprise seriously, while France looked upon it as a "side issue" as compared with the dynastic struggle on the continent of Europe between the Bourbons and the Hapsburgs, the chief significance of this century-long contest was that it represented a struggle between two different colonial systems—the intensive occupation and exploitation of a limited area versus the extremely meager occupation of a vast territory by a few soldiers and traders. In 1688 there were about 300,000 English colonists in the narrow Piedmont region of the Atlantic Coast, while there were scarcely 20,000 Frenchmen in the vast regions of Canada and the Mississippi Valley. With the French further handicapped by futile dissipation of energy elsewhere and infinitely weaker in colonial policy, there could be only one issue to the conflict, and by the Treaty of Paris of 1763, Great Britain took over the possession of the great majority of the French colonies in America.

But this very triumph of Great Britain over her traditional European enemy only involved her in a more serious struggle with her most aggressive colonial domains, the English colonies of the Atlantic Coast. The occupation of the vast territory conquered from France west of the Alleghenies forced upon England a reconstruction of her hitherto loosely organized and indifferently enforced colonial policy. This imperial organization necessitated additional expenditures, which Great Britain proposed to raise through direct taxation and through enforcement of the long dormant navigation laws. But this fiscal policy aroused the opposition of the colonial merchants, long accustomed to unhampered smuggling, and they united with the debtor landlords of the Southern colonies to give vitality to that aspiration for

independence which Sydney George Fisher has analyzed with such
acumen. The revolution that ensued was in its essence a civil war
within the British Empire, in which British and American liberals made
common cause against conservatives and imperialists in both countries. The colonial cause prevailed chiefly on account of that defec-
tion of the British Whigs which George Macaulay Trevelyan, John Fiske
and William Edward Hartpole Lecky have clearly recognized and described and through French aid begotten of the spirit of revenge for
the defeat of 1756-1763.

The loss of the more important British colonies in America produced a marked tendency toward the granting of greater autonomy to
the British colonies that remained. This changing attitude was re-
flected in the Quebec Acts of 1774 and 1791, the Irish Parliament Act
of 1782 and the India Act of 1784. But the thoroughgoing revision of
British imperial policy in a liberal direction did not take place until a
half-century later, following Lord Durham's [John George Lambton] famous Canada report of 1839.

In this first phase of European expansion Germany [The Great
Elector of Bradenburg established a few posts on the west coast of
Africa.—Ed.], Austria and Russia failed to participate—Germany because of distracting religious wars and Austria and Russia on account
of isolation, inertia or propinquity to a vast amount of unoccupied districts in Asia. The fact that they remained outside the circle of the new
commercial and colonial powers was most important in determining
the lines of their later political and economic evolution, and possessed
the greatest significance for their subsequent history and for that of
the rest of the world. It should not be forgotten, however, that Russia
was beginning that expansion eastward through Siberia which was to
make her an important participant in the second great period of colonial expansion, namely, that after 1870. Even in the 18th century she
established
outposts in Alaska.

While it has been important in this preliminary section to call attention to the colonial activities of the European states that partici-
pated in this process of expansion, by far the most significant aspect

of European expansion from 1500 to 1800 lay in the reaction of European contacts abroad upon European society itself. It is with these various phases of the reaction of expansion upon European conditions that we shall concern ourselves in the remainder of our discussion.

An artist's rendering of a compass and an astrolabe, two of the inventions that revolutionized sea travel and made the Age of Exploration possible.

CHAPTER FIVE

The Outstanding Aspects Of the Origins of Western Civilization: Improvements in Navigation And Ship-Building

Perhaps the most striking immediate effect of the expansion of Europe was its influence upon European and world commerce. The results in this field constitute what is, narrowly and technically speaking, the Commercial Revolution, though it has been the practice of many historians to use this term to designate the whole process of the growth of extra-European commerce, the rise of the capitalistic age, and the multiplicity of economic, social, political and intellectual results flowing therefrom.

The whole era of expansion and commercial development rested upon certain important improvements in the art of navigation. In the first place, there was the series of inventions in the field of nautical instruments, from the earlier compass and astrolabe to the chronometer in the 18th century. The provision of quadrant and sextant, telescopes and other accessories enabled mariners to find their way at sea far more safely and effectively than had ever been the case in early maritime activity. Maps, charts and tables were constantly improved, lighthouses built, harbors cleared of natural obstacles, and pilot services inaugurated. The rise of national governments marked the end of medieval strand laws, which had practically conferred upon localities the right to pillage stranded vessels.

Along with these improvements went the development of larger and more seaworthy ships. At first the tendency was to concentrate upon improvement in size, and we have the development of the galleon and the carrack, vessels of from two to five decks, exceedingly well armed to beat off privateers and pirates. Ships of this sort were, however, rather unwieldy, and the Dutch and British specialized in craft somewhat small in size, but far swifter, more seaworthy and more reliable. The Commercial Revolution rests upon these inventions and improvements connected with the art of navigation, much as the later Industrial Revolution depended upon inventions in textile machinery, steam power and metallurgy.

"The whole era of expansion and commercial development rested upon certain important improvements in the art of navigation. In the first place, there was the series of inventions in the field of nautical instruments, from the earlier compass and astrolabe to the chronometer in the 18th century."

ego velivolis ambivi cursibus Orbe
Magellane novo te duce ducta freto.

An illustration of the 85-ton carrack *Victoria*, one of the vessels used by Ferdinand Magellan to circumnavigate the globe, circa 1510-1519.

CHAPTER SIX

Increase in
The Volume
Of Trade

The first notable phase of the Commercial Revolution was the great increase in the volume of trade. Hitherto the trade of Europe with the rest of the world had been limited rather strictly to the products of the Orient, chiefly spices, silks, tapestries, precious stones, perfume, woods and commodities of this sort; most of them, with the notable exception of the spices, being articles of luxury rather than articles of common consumption. With the discovery of the new areas, particularly in the New World and the East Indies, the supply of these articles was greatly increased and a whole new range of commodities added.

The European demand steadily increased for such things as tea, coffee, cocoa and other beverages of this sort; for Jamaican rum; for sugar; for various types of vegetable foodstuffs such as potatoes, lima beans, tapioca and yams; for tropical fruit—for example, lemons, limes, oranges, bananas and pineapples; for carpets, rugs, wall paper, eastern furniture and china; for new forms of Oriental dress and adornment, ostrich feathers, furs from the colder regions; for drugs and medications—chiefly in the form of herbs and extracts; and, above all, for tobacco, which vied with sugar as the largest single element in the European imports from the New World for a considerable period of time. Perishable tropical fruits which could not be successfully shipped prior to the rise of maritime refrigerators were introduced and grown in southern Europe and northern Africa.

For early modern times there are no trade statistics broad enough in scope and compiled with sufficient care and understanding to be worth quoting. We have to visualize the extent of economic progress chiefly in other ways. By 1700 Europe's habits of consumption were vastly changed by the influx of new goods. Upper-class life was profoundly affected by 1600, but the amount of innovation varied greatly from one locality to another. The new states had not yet achieved highly organized or unified economic systems, and internal lines of communication were still poor for the most part. By 1700, middle classes, particularly in England, Holland, Spain and Portugal, had generally changed the mode and standards of consumption, but the laborious masses of people were still living much as in the Middle Ages. It was not until the 18th century that the effects of the Commercial Revolution penetrated to the very foundations of European society, producing a so-called "Industrial Revolution" which has altered the conditions of human life more than any other event in history.

In spite of her naval defeat at the hands of England, a half-century before, the Netherlands remained at the opening of the 18th century one of the most important commercial states. Not until the middle of the 18th century did England surpass her in the economic enterprise of Europe. Though dislodged from her primacy by 1800, the Netherlands persisted as a prominent state in the commerce and carrying trade of the world.

While inferior to the Dutch in commercial power and activity in the 17th century, England was already beginning that commercial and manufacturing development which was to place her in a position of undisputed leadership in the industry and trade of the Old World. At the end of the 17th century England was importing about $17 million worth of goods annually and exporting goods to the value of $32 million. This trade increased about six-fold within 100 years. The total foreign commerce of France appears to have been somewhat smaller at the earlier date—her economic life had just been disastrously affected by a series of religious civil wars and the destruction or emigration of a large part of her most desirable industrial population, the Huguenot craftsmen. Her foreign trade increased in volume at about the same rate as that of England, but somewhat less rapidly in the overseas commodities. England began dealing with the lands across the sea, coming more and more to import raw materials and export manufactured goods. France's trade remained chiefly with her European neighbors, and over two-thirds of her exports were raw materials. Her American trade in 1716 was only some $5 million; that with Asia and Africa combined about $2.5 million—and all three taken together amounted to only about a fifth of her business with the European countries.

England ultimately achieved an enormous economic superiority because the future lay with the two lines of activity she was beginning to cultivate: overseas trade and manufacturing. While the commercial changes in English life were prophetic of the future, it must be borne in mind that they took place gradually. In 1700, England's overseas trade amounted to but 21% of her total foreign trade, while that of France in 1716 totalled 18%. Seventy years later proportions were in each case respectively 40% and 33%. But the expansion of trade and the growing ascendancy of exports over imports were a definite and striking process.

The situation at the opening of the 18th century is very well illustrated by coffee, a commodity very rarely used in Europe a century earlier. Consumption doubled between 1710 and 1720, and again in the following decade; but in the next five years, 1730-1735, it almost tripled. The breakfast table of the middle classes was already a fact. Coffee is only a suggestive illustration of the general situation—cloth was to prove far more important because importation was destined to give way to manufacture. Cloth-making was to bring iron and coal to the fore, and these have revolutionized the modern world.

In the 17th century England had a large trade in salt fish with the south Atlantic colonies and the West Indies. With the Southern colonies she had a highly developed tobacco and rice trade and had laid the foundations for a flourishing commerce in naval stores. She did a lucrative fur business with the North Atlantic colonies and the Hudson Bay region. She imported from the North Atlantic colonies iron, lumber, codfish and oil. With the West Indies she had an immense trade in sugar, molasses, rum, dyes, spices, cotton, tropical woods and tobacco. She divided with the Dutch a slave trade between the western coast of Africa and the American colonies. West Africa also furnished gold, gum-arabic, ebony, rare woods, ostrich feathers and ivory. From the Far East and the East Indies she imported an impressive list of commodities thus described by a contemporary writer:

> Books, canes, drugs, gums, oils, indigo in large quantities, cochineal, China-ink, galls turmeric, seedlack, stricklack, ivory, fans, cane-mats, cinnamon, cloves, mace, nutmeg, pepper, cayenne pepper, ginger, sago, sugar, tea, rice, coffee, preserved fruits, mother-of-pearl shell, and spoons made of it, saltpeter, arrack, cotton, cotton yarn, raw silk of Bengal and China, calicoes and muslins, cassia, ebony, sandal, satin and sapan woods, porcelains, japanned cabinets, ornamental furniture, tiger skins and precious stones.

Set off against these imports from overseas were the leading English exports of wheat, woolen and cotton cloth, hardware, gunpowder and various trinkets which were used in the trade with backward peoples.

"By 1700, middle classes, particularly in England, Holland, Spain and Portugal, had generally changed the mode and standards of consumption, but the laborious masses of people were still living much as in the Middle Ages."

Of the thousands of depictions of ancient Egyptian ships, only three illustrate seagoing vessels. One is a relief in the mortuary temple at Deir el Bahri of Queen Hatshepsut. This ancient relief depicts Egyptian sailors on such a vessel.

CHAPTER SEVEN

Widened Geographic Scope Of Trading Operations

A ccompanying this marked development in the volume and variety of European trade there was a revolutionary change in the geographic scope of trading operations. In the earliest period of trade, it was carried on primarily in river basins. This stage of civilization has been called by some writers the "fluvial." Shortly after the dawn of recorded history, some daring navigators had so far mastered the art of navigation as to venture upon the great inland seas. This trade, from the Egyptian and Aegean commerce of the 4th millennium B.C. to that around the Mediterranean in the Middle Ages, has been called "thalassic," meaning commerce along the coast of an inland sea. In the period of European expansion overseas the commerce of the western world passed from the thalassic type, which had endured for some 5,000 years, to the stage of oceanic or worldwide traffic. Only a relatively small portion of the habitable parts of the world was touched by explorers during this earlier period, but they enormously extended the range of European geographic knowledge and contacts and laid the foundations for the colonization and discoveries of the 19th century. The whole period of four centuries since 1500 has been relatively brief, but it has opened up to western Europe the majority of the land area of the planet. Many careful thinkers, even those most hostile to modern life as compared with that of the ancient world at its best, have seized upon this world-wide system of transportation and intercommunication as the most characteristic aspect of present-day civilization.

This illustration, entitled "Trade on the Sea-ports of the Levant," was based upon a miniature in a manuscript of *The Travels of Marco Polo* (15th century) from the Library of the Arsenal of Paris.

CHAPTER EIGHT

Growing Supremacy of Western Seaboard Towns

As overseas exploration gathered way, chiefly under the leadership of the towns and states of the Atlantic seaboard of Europe, the centers of commercial activity were no longer Genoa, Pisa, Amalfi or Venice, but Lisbon, Seville, Cadiz, Bordeaux, Nantes, Dieppe, Dunkirk, St. Milo, Antwerp, Amsterdam, Bristol, Liverpool and London. The shift of commercial domination from the Mediterranean to the northwest was more than a mere economic change. It meant that new cities were to become the dominant factors in the history of mankind in the West; that the Mediterranean world, dominant for five millennia, would retire to a position of second-rate significance. Henceforth, for several centuries, the basic orientation of Europe was to be mainly toward the west, with the great area of development located in northwestern Europe and the newly discovered continents. While the Near East was to remain significant for western Europe from the days of the Turkish siege of Vienna to those of the Suez Canal, the Baghdad Railroad, and the partitions of Persia, it lost its position of primary commercial importance.

A collection of Spanish coins.

CHAPTER NINE

Increased Supply
Of Precious Metals

No less revolutionary than the commercial changes were those connected with the development of new financial situations and methods. There was, of course, a very intimate and causal relationship between the rise of the new commerce and the development of the capitalistic age. Down to the time of overseas expansion there had been, as already noted, a great scarcity of precious metals in Europe. This had been an inevitable outcome of the situation late in the Middle Ages when Europe had depended upon the Orient for both money and the more expensive goods. The only practicable way to keep goods flowing westward was to find either money or goods to flow eastward in exchange. Europeans had made increasingly successful efforts to duplicate or find substitutes for the Oriental imports, to mine and mint money, and to develop products of their own to exchange in the Oriental trade. At the opening of the 16th century the money situation was already somewhat ameliorated. Europe was producing some $500,000 to $750,000 a year in precious metals, and a similar amount was being drawn from the west coast of Africa. If we accept the usual estimates of $170 million to $200 million as the amount of coinage in circulation in Europe in 1492 or 1500, $250 million is not an improbable figure for 1520. Accumulation went on constantly in spite of the drain eastward, and both European and African production of precious metals was being stimulated in every possible way. This acceleration in output continued to about 1600, after which time the dearth of money was somewhat less acute and the flood of gold and silver from America had so raised prices and wages as to render many Old World mines unprofitable. In addition to the gold and silver in circulation as coinage about 1520, there was also a considerable amount in the form of plate and other works of art, and much was hoarded in the form of bars, coins etc. Nothing much better than a blind guess at the total would be possible.

The usual estimate is probably conservative enough—that the coinage of Europe increased about twelvefold during the 16th century. Though the general anticipation as to the volume of precious metals available in the New World was far greater than the actuality, and many Europeans spent their lives in fruitless search for mountains of gold and silver, the actual amount brought into Europe by the close of the 18th century was stupendous in comparison with that existing in 1500. Spain had access to more and richer mines than the other European states, but the latter, particularly England, were able to remove this handicap to some degree by depredations upon Spanish commerce and the seizure of scores of richly laden treasure ships.

"No less revolutionary than the commercial changes were those connected with the development of new financial situations and methods."

Hall of Merchants' Company of York, England. Originally published in Lambert's *Two Thousand Years of Gild Life*, published by A. Brown & Sons, Hull.

CHAPTER TEN

Dislocation of Prices

G old and silver being commodities, they follow the general rule that an increase in supply is accompanied by a roughly proportional decrease in exchange value against other goods. This proportion must not be rigidly applied, of course, even to the 16th century, since a standard medium of exchange, though itself a commodity, occupies a very special position in the economic order. We must not be surprised, therefore, to find that the increase in money metals is not exactly parallel or relative to that of prices and wages, from year to year or even from decade to decade. Nearly all economic tendencies require a certain amount of time to express themselves and they are usually counteracted, retarded, or reinforced by other factors, among which the deliberate purposes of men are often not the least potent.

This great increase in prices due to increased specie and demand for goods had many important economic and social results. In the first place, it greatly stimulated trade and speculation, culminating the disastrous period of "bubbles." It increased considerably the profits of the industrial and merchant classes and wage-earners. In general, however, salaried and wage-earning people suffered because their stipends could not be increased as rapidly as the cost of living. This was particularly true of the wage-earners in those states where the guild system still persisted, for the rules of the guild prevented any very significant increase in the wages paid for the labor of journeymen. The landed nobility who received their rent payments on long-term leases in kind were much less adversely affected than those who had reduced the dues to cash, since the price of farm produce increased, while the purchasing power of a given amount of money fell off. The squires who owned and worked their own farms tended to share in the prosperity because of the remarkable rise in the prices of the things they had to sell. Long term leaseholders tended to profit at the expense of their landlords, due to the fact that while their rents remained unchanged, the income from the land increased with the rise in prices. In many instances governments took cognizance of these price changes and attempted legal regulation but, as in the old Statutes of Laborers, such opposition to general economic tendencies was usually unsuccessful. Gradually the European situation became adjusted to the larger amount of precious metal and to the corresponding changes in price levels. In general, the net result of both was greatly to stimulate economic activity and achievement.

"Gold and silver being commodities, they follow the general rule that an increase in supply is accompanied by a roughly proportional decrease in exchange value against other goods. A standard medium of exchange, though itself a commodity, occupies a very special position in the economic order."

Illustration of Anton Fugger by Hans Maeir zu Schwarz, 1530. Art Gallery, Karlsube.

CHAPTER ELEVEN

The Beginning Of Modern Capitalism

One of the most striking and characteristic phases of the development of the modern order was the beginning of what is commonly called modern capitalism, namely, the creation of relatively large fortunes available for various types of economic enterprise. Along with the growth of private capital there went, of course, a marked increase in the income of the state, private and public capitalism thus developing together. The accumulation of working capital on a large scale, according to our standards, first took place in early modern times. While there was some approximation to a capitalistic regime in ancient Babylonia, nothing like the situation of even the 17th century in Europe existed in the ancient Orient. In both Greece and Rome, the agrarian economy, rather than the capitalistic outlook, prevailed. There was relatively little development of the concept or practice of accumulating money power for the furtherance of economic expansion. Italian financial organization in the late Middle Ages was more like modern capitalism in many respects, but most of the great banking houses were family ventures, their capital was much less than that of modern concerns of equal repute and current traditions and practices greatly hampered their operations.

Too much of the earlier prejudice against interest remained, the rates were high and erratic, and the question of proper security was still unsolved. Many of the banks succumbed through the defalcation of princes too strong to be coerced. Others decayed with the families which controlled them, because the joint-stock company was not yet well enough worked out to bring in new blood and drop outlived policies. The Peruzzis of the 14th century had a capital of some $800,000, the Medicis of the 15th perhaps $7.5 million. The Fuggers of southern Germany had many times as much, but the period of their greatest prosperity belongs to early modern rather than late medieval times. Their capital at the peak of their prosperity has been estimated at $40 million. In Europe generally, and especially in northern Europe, in the medieval period, the industrial limitations of the guild system, the lack of extensive and varied commerce and the attitude of the church toward interest had greatly limited the application of capital, and hence its accumulation. It required the era of overseas expansion, with the remarkable growth of commercial activity and the accompanying revolutionary discoveries of precious metals to create modern capitalism. Moreover, the decay of the manorial and guild systems made labor marketable in a new sense, injecting an element of mobility and adaptability which was unique at least in degree.

More than any other criterion in the economic field, capitalism separates the modern and contemporary era from the ancient and medieval ages. Certain statistics which have been gathered with respect to England in the 17th century well illustrate this tendency toward a marked increase of available capital. The estimated national wealth of England in 1600 was £17 million; in 1630, £28 million; in 1660, £56 million; and in 1688, £88 million. Equally illuminating is the increase of coin in England during this same period. In 1600 it is estimated that the extant coin in England was some £4 million; in 1625, £6 million; in 1660, £16 million; and in 1680, £18.5 million. The royal income also showed a remarkable development, particularly from the customs dues. In 1603 the customs dues of England amounted to only £36,000; by 1660, they had increased to over £400,000. A generation or so after this time, at the height of the prosperity of the East India Company, this great organization alone paid an annual tribute to the English treasury of some £400,000. It is estimated that the annual income of William III in 1700 was £4,415,360.

Private fortunes, of considerable size—many of them totaling over £1 million—were also built up at this time, in part through privateering and in part through speculation and investment in commercial manufacturing activity. In the latter part of the 16th century, especially privateering, was a lucrative enterprise. The voyage of Drake in 1577-1580 brought in a spoil of some £600,000, of which around £275,000 was handed over to the Queen as the share of the state in this form of semi-legalized piracy. Besides the private fortunes accumulated through speculation in stocks, many enriched themselves through graft in positions with the government or with trading organizations, most notorious being the "nabobs" in the East Indian service. Others amassed considerable sums as resident planters or absentee landlords of the New World, particularly in the West Indies. It should not, of course, be assumed that all of the fortunes accumulated in the 17th and 18th centuries were the product of dubious or illegitimate enterprises. Many more rose from the ranks of labor solely as the result of energy, application and sagacity in constructive business and commercial ventures. The case of William Miles, as described by Botsford, is representative of this large class.

This young man came to Bristol with three halfpence, obtained a job as a porter, and did evening work for a small shipbuilder. On the completion of his apprenticeship, by which he had saved £15, he qualified as a ship's carpenter in a Jamaica merchantman. There he bought a cask or two of sugar, which he sold in Bristol at a huge profit. With this money he stocked up articles in greatest demand in Jamaica, and repeated his former investment. Saving his earnings, which became larger each trip, he settled down in Bristol as a sugar-merchant, in which capacity he amassed a large fortune. In 1793, his son joined him in partnership, not only in the West India trade, but in the largest sugar-refining business in Bristol.... The capitalist manufacturer was also, in general, a self-made man; and curiously enough, few who entered the trade rich were successful. The men who did establish them-

selves were raised by their own efforts, commencing
in a very humble way, and pushing their advance by a
series of unceasing exertions, having a very limited
capital to begin with, or even none at all save that of
their own labor. [Botsford, 120, 124.—Ed.]

While the fortunes of this age were insignificant as compared to
those of the late 19th and the 20th centuries, they far exceeded anything which had been previously known in Europe, if not in the history of mankind. It is, to be sure, something more than the mere size
of the fortunes which characterizes modern capitalism. The extent of
monetary possessions alone would scarcely distinguish Crassus from
the Fuggers. Even more important was the changing conception of
the nature of capital and its possible uses, particularly investment, in
the expansion of business enterprises. The "theory of business enterprise" and the "price-system" gradually triumphed over the attitudes
and conceptions of the napkin and agrarian economy—an epoch-mak-
ing transition which has received its classic analysis, from differing
points of view, at the hands of Weber, Werner Sombart, Veglen, See and
Hobson. Very important also was the de-personalization of business
forces and instruments. The distinction gradually developed between
the capital and assets of a business unit and the capital and assets of
the individuals involved or concerned. Neither the Greeks nor the Flo-
rentines had even been able to achieve this dissociation, which
emerged as a result of the transition from a need-covering economy,
based on ideas of necessity and the just-price, to economic life
founded on the aspirations to make the utmost possible pecuniary
profit.

By the close of the 16th century the last vestiges of the medieval
prejudice against interest had been swept away. The new need for
working capital was the most important factor in producing this result. Long before the Protestant Revolt the church had ceased to in-
veigh against interest as such, but had retained earnest convictions
about extortionate rates and various abuses of wealth which were regarded as at variance with the Christian religion. For good or ill, reli-

gious authority was weakened by the Reformation at a most critical time. Europe went through a religious and an economic revolution at the same time, with both religious camps needing all the moral and financial support they could get. In the long run, the Christian Church as a whole—if we may speak of it thus after the Protestant Revolt— probably settled down more smoothly and complacently to the new capitalistic system than would have been the case without the 16th-century theological upheaval to distract its attention from economic matters during the critical years of the transition.

The decisive factor in creating a new attitude toward interest-taking was the demand for large sums of working capital for investment in overseas trading ventures and in the larger business units in Europe which grew up with them. It was impossible, as we now see, to accumulate this capital without offering some reward. Not only were the timeworn economic ideals of Aristotle and the medieval church abandoned, but the banking class, deriving its income largely from interest, was raised to a position of peculiar eminence and respect. Obviously, there was nothing brand-new or astonishing about this—it was merely the result of the growth and spread, under exceptionally favorable circumstances, of a condition clearly visible in the medieval Italian towns.

An important aspect of the rise of capitalism and new business instruments and methods was the growth and fixation of the idea of the business-unit, firm or enterprise.

The Money Changer & His Wife by Marinus van Reymer-Swaele, 1539, Museo del Prado, Madrid, Spain.

CHAPTER TWELVE

The Rise of Banking

T he roots of the modern banking system reach back to the Jewish and Syrian moneychangers of the medieval towns and fairs. They were mere transplantations from the more complicated economic order of the eastern Mediterranean region, where their origins are lost to antiquity. The craft of goldsmiths played an important part in the shifting of this financial power from non-Christians to Christians, particularly the Lombard and Caursine moneychangers. The goldsmith's strongbox or guarded house, the wide financial organization for papal collections, and the collaboration of the older non-Christian money power in the fairs and the Near Eastern trade following the opening of the Crusades, led to the establishment of a public bank in Venice in 1171. Florence later became the great banking center because of the papal collections and its foreign trade, particularly in cloth and the materials for making cloth. A bank was opened in Delft in 1313, one at Calais in 1320 and a third at Geneva in 1345. The bank of Barcelona, opened in 1401, was a still closer approximation to the modern banking institution and the famous St. George organization in Genoa was consolidated in 1407.

During the 15th century, northern and central Europeans encroached more and more upon the banking monopoly of the Lombards. Northern Europe's superior natural resources made it potentially a vastly richer country than the Mediterranean region—an embarrassment of unrealized wealth which had already played its part in loosening the bonds of the Roman Empire. Throughout the Middle Ages the peopling of northern Europe and the development of such variegated resources in so many places delayed the consolidation of the new or "modern" order, while, at the same time, its enormous unfolding possibilities prevented an effectual resuscitation of the old.

The remarkable development of northwestern Europe was as much a cause as an effect of the expansion of European civilization. By 1500, the Fuggers of Augsburg, well north of the Alps, were the richest banking house in Europe. They had erected their business largely through the aid of Bohemian, Styrian, and Carinthian gold. Already, in 1511, before their section of Europe had become seriously involved in overseas ventures, they had a capital of 186,760 gulden, a sum which had increased to 2,021,202 gulden [Representing a purchasing power of more than $10 million in our money. This figure must be practically doubled for the peak of their prosperity, about 1546.—Ed.] by 1527. At this time, they were making about 55% annually on their investments. The great period of the development of modern banking came, however, after the opening of the 17th century. By this time all western Europe was beginning to feel the results of the new overseas trade, and was laying the foundation for the remarkable development of industry and commerce which was to characterize this region. The following are among the more important banks that were established from the opening of the 17th century to the close of the 18th century:

> Bank of Amsterdam, 1607
> Bank of Middelburg, 1616
> Bank of Venice, 1619
> Bank of Hamburg, 1619
> Bank of Rotterdam, 1635
> Bank of Sweden, 1656
> Bank of Spain, 1665
> Bank of England, 1694
> Bank of Vienna, 1703
> Bank of Berlin and Breslau, 1765

These banks made possible the systematic accumulation of capital to be put at the disposal of enterprising merchants and manufacturers, facilitated loans, began the process of discounting commercial paper, and in other ways rendered more effective the various financial aids to industry and commerce. To be sure, even the greatest of the 17th and 18th century banks were relatively insignificant compared with the larger ones in a second-class American city of today. Few loaned money at first to manufacturers or engaged in a personal loan business, but they formed the beginnings out of which have grown such establishments as those of Speyer, Rothschild, Morgan, and no less imposing quasi-public concerns like the Bank of England. The development of banking made possible the beginning of the issuance of various types of commercial paper which is indispensable to modern exchange, either national or international. Among these were promissory notes, drafts, and bills of exchange. Important also for business operations of the newer sort was Pacciuolis' invention of modern double-entry bookkeeping.

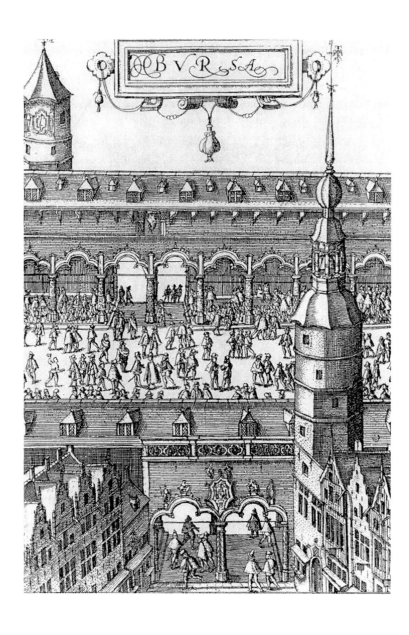

An engraving of the Antwerp Stock Exchange, circa 1650, a *Bird's Eye View* of the building that was destroyed in 1858.

CHAPTER THIRTEEN

The Rise of Produce
And Stock Exchanges

Important produce exchanges grew up in Antwerp and Amsterdam during the 16th century, supplementing the work of the banking system. The Antwerp exchange was perhaps the greatest trading center up to that time in the history of Europe. In both of the two mentioned the practice developed of making exchanges by the use of paper securities, instead of the more cumbersome method of trading in the actual commodities. To make this possible it was necessary to create an elaborate system of grading and supervision, to ensure the correspondence of the paper instruments to specific kinds as well as amounts of goods. An inevitable accompaniment of this innovation was the appearance of the first general tendency toward speculation in paper securities. In addition to facilitating the exchange of commodities, these produce exchanges broadened the opportunities for borrowing and investing money.

With the growth of new business enterprises and commercial companies on the joint-stock basis appeared the need for an organized agency through which the shares of stock might be sold, bought or exchanged. For a long time this function was performed by the produce exchange. The two gradually become differentiated, and in our time the stock exchange is a distinct institution. By the end of the 17th century the joint-stock company had generally reached the state of freely transferable shares, but businessmen did not fully appreciate the possible uses and abuses of the stock exchange as an instrument of investment and speculation. It required the great inflations and disasters of the "bubble" period in the first quarter of the 18th century to give people some idea of the limitations within which it is safe to use paper instruments in place of things. The services of the bourses to the joint-stock companies were, to be sure, far less extensive in the 17th and 18th centuries than they became in the 19th. Their speculative activity was largely confined to public loans which were the favorite form of investment down to the 19th century, when the canal and railway companies began to put their securities on the market. The trading companies were usually able to sell their bonds successfully through private channels.

The first true stock exchange resembling the modern type was established in London in 1698. It was followed by one in Paris in 1724. The first one set up in America was opened in New York City in 1817. As in our own day, the stock exchange helped along both good and bad practices. In helping to gather large quantities of capital for profitable investment, it aided in a highly valuable constructive function, but it also invited chicanery and foolish speculation. Yet, in spite of the great abuses, there is no doubt that the stock exchanges did much to stimulate and carry along the development of the great trading companies of the 17th and 18th centuries.

"The first true stock exchange resembling the modern type was established in London in 1698. It was followed by one in Paris in 1724. The first one set up in America was opened in New York City in 1817. As in our own day, the stock exchange helped along both good and bad practices."

Cover illustration by Frank E. Schoonover (1877-1972) for *The Privateers of '76* (Philadelphia: Penn Publishing Co., 1923), oil on canvas, from the University of Delaware Permanent Collection, gift of the John R. McFarlin Memorial Fund, First Regional Art Exhibition, 1962.

CHAPTER FOURTEEN

The Rise of Insurance

Insurance companies existed in Italian cities at the end of the Middle Ages. The more extensive maritime enterprises of the 16th century involved a greater amount of risk on account of the varied dangers of ocean travel, including pirates and privateers as well as storms and accidents. Insurance against loss in speculative companies was also desirable. It was in line with the great development of collective enterprise to spread out the risks among a number of people, so that all would lose a little instead of one losing everything. One simple way of accomplishing this was by means of an agreement among cooperating merchants—a written contract to distribute any losses incurred in the enterprise contemplated. All would sign their names beneath the agreement, from which practice arose the term "underwriting." Greater specialization and organization were inevitable as business grew more complicated. Merchants developed the habit of meeting, for example, in the great coffee houses of London, especially at Lloyd's, and arranging for the insurance of ships. The next step was the organization of insurance companies which specialized in this type of business. Such companies became relatively well systematized by the opening of the 18th century, and the business tended to gravitate into the hands of a few more powerful and efficient insurance companies.

In England, by 1725, the London and the Royal Insurance Companies had a virtual monopoly on the insurance business with the English merchants. While maritime insurance did not develop so extensively in other European countries as in England, progress along roughly similar lines took place in all those states which shared in the overseas trade. Other forms of insurance appeared at about the same

time or a little later. There was no important development of fire insurance companies until after the great fire of 1660 in London. This
was followed by the organization of a number of fire insurance companies, the first on a joint-stock basis (1681). The Sun Fire Company,
which opened its offices in 1706, was the first to carry on business on
a large scale. Life insurance companies appeared during this same period. As in the case of fire insurance, individuals had carried on a
crude and sporadic business for some time and a mutual company, the
Friendly Society, was organized in 1684 but he first great companies
were the Amicable (1706) and the Equitable (1762), both historic English concerns still in existence.

"In England, by 1725, the London and the Royal Insurance Companies had a virtual monopoly on the insurance business with the English merchants."

Whale-Fishing, a woodcut in the *Cosmographic Universelle of Thevet*, Paris, 1574.

CHAPTER FIFTEEN

The Rise of Speculation
And 'Bubbles'

The new opportunities for gain and the rise of the profit-getting objective produced an orgy of speculation at the close of the 17th and opening of the 18th century. This age possessed all the love of pecuniary accumulation that exists today, but was without the more chastened attitudes and methods that have been produced by the lessons of a couple of centuries of disappointment and loss from unwise and over-optimistic investments. This speculative spirit of the period is well described by Professor G.W. Botsford:

> The psychology of the *nouveaux riches* may be perceived by an understanding of their business ethics. The easiest and quickest way to make money was by speculation in the stock market. The buying and selling of stock, of course, more closely resembled gambling than the exchange of legitimate securities. There were no financial experts to enlighten popular ignorance with accurate knowledge; nor was there a vigilant board of directors to expose shams or legislation to prevent the foisting of fraudulent stock on the public. On the contrary, every means was taken to fascinate the public mind by vague rumors of imaginary advantages. False reports of fabulous profits were seemingly substantiated by dividends which could never be paid from legitimate gains. Particularly in

the case of the South Sea hoax, and of the thousand
and one lesser bubbles, did the government share the
blame, with the stock-jobbers themselves, for the stimulation of human cupidity. [Botsford, 162-162.—Ed.]

The most famous of the manias of speculation of the 40 years or
so up to 1720 were the English "South Sea Bubble" and the even more
sensational aftermath of John Law's financial experiment in France,
sometimes called the "Mississippi Bubble."

The English South Sea Trading Company was organized in 1711,
with a capital of £10 million ($50 million), all of which was loaned to
the government at eight percent.

Under the terms of the Treaty of Utrecht (1713) the English obtained a monopoly on the slave trade with the Spanish-American
colonies, and also the right to send one shipload of merchandise per
year. Both privileges were handed over to the South Sea Company. It
added whale-fishing and other legitimate ventures to its activities. In
1720, it offered to take over a national debt of some £32 million at five
percent, instead of the six and eight percent rates the government had
been paying.

The share-holders exchanged their holdings for stock in the company and all seemed to be going well until the public got a sudden
passion for the shares and bid them up to 10 times their actual value
on the basis of the interest they drew. The dividends of the company
being only seven or eight percent, those who bought the shares at a
1,000 percent of their face value were naturally ruined.

This was only one of a number of stock enterprises floated at the
time, most of them bogus. People bought shares in enterprises for
making perpetual motion machines, for putting alchemy on a commercial basis, for exploiting "gold mines" in the Carolinas, for developing
fisheries in Greenland, importing walnut trees from Virginia and even,
in one case, "for an undertaking which shall in due time be revealed."
A general crash followed. The force of these crises is broken in various
ways but preventing them is still outside the realm of practical
achievement. So far as anyone can say now, they may be an inevitable

part of the price we must pay for the advantages of using paper instruments to represent things, and of producing goods for markets we hope to find at distant times and places.

Wall painting from the head offices of the British East India Company. The company was granted an English Royal Charter by Elizabeth I on Dec. 31, 1600 for trade privileges in India. The Royal Charter effectively gave the newly created Honorable East India Company a 21-year monopoly on all trade in the East Indies. The company transformed from a commercial trading venture to one that virtually ruled India as it acquired auxiliary governmental and military functions, until its dissolution in 1858.

CHAPTER SIXTEEN

The Sudden Rise of Commercial Monopolies

A leading characteristic of the new overseas trade, handled by large and well-knit companies, was the tendency toward commercial monopolies of the trade in certain areas, in specific commodities or both. In the first place, there was the obvious advantage to the company itself which dominated the trade in a particular commodity. Furthermore, since the sources of such goods were rather limited and specific, it was relatively easy to maintain a monopoly by controlling the supply at its origin. The company which first developed contacts with an area had an enormous advantage in its trade, particularly when its position was strengthened by government favoritism.

In most European states, monopoly was encouraged and developed by the attitude of the governments. Trading monopolies were favored because of the greater ease and certainty of governmental control over the activities of merchants, a few companies being far easier to supervise than a cloud of independent traders. The friendliness of governments toward great monopolies was also due in part to the belief that this was the way to foster and encourage commerce, one of the leading aims of the states under the mercantilist theory of the time.

As a result of these various influences, among others, commercial monopolies became the usual thing in the 17th and 18th centuries, and monopoly was a basic element in the organization and activities of the early trading companies.

Stained glass window depicts Luther nailing his 99 theses to the door of Wittenberg Church.

CHAPTER SEVENTEEN

Mercantilism and
The Absolute State

The commercial expansion of this age (1500-1800) with its various subordinate results, had a direct and important effect upon the political tendencies of the time, particularly the growth of large territorial states and the trend toward secular absolutism. With the increased resources of the royal treasuries, as a result of income from privateering, customs duties, fees for chartering monopolistic companies etc, the kings became more powerful, and were able gradually to make good their aspiration for ascendancy over feudal lords. The possibility of maintaining a paid, loyal army and officialdom was a basic factor in creating the early national dynastic states. This income was also used by many states in warfare to extend their holdings in Europe and overseas. Again, the various activities of the state in connection with commercial monopolies and maritime regulation served greatly to extend the notion of its importance and the scope of its activities. The narrowly conceived commercial policy known as Mercantilism served to create a feeling of national separatism and jealously, thus stimulating the nationalistic trend in this new age. Finally, the Protestant schism in the church, the great international institution of the Middle Ages, partially removed one of the principal checks upon the growth of secular absolutism.

The Commercial Revolution produced a very important development in the commercial theories and policies of western Europe. Interference by central governments in economic life had not been unknown in the medieval period, but the weakness of the secular state had prevented such control from assuming any very significant proportions. With the combined and parallel growth of world commerce and the national dynastic state, there evolved the policy and practice of the most complete governmental regulation of economic activities. This new policy, though varying in detail and extent of application, was known as Mercantilism in England, as Colbertism in France, and as Cameralism in Germany. It rested upon the projection into economic life of the existing narrowly nationalistic conceptions and practices. Every state was assumed to be the potential commercial enemy of every other, and the prosperity of each was supposed to depend upon a narrow exclusive policy of monopolizing the trade of its colonies and, at the same time, doing everything possible to restrict or injure the commerce of its neighbors.

The fundamental assumptions of this mercantilist system were roughly as follows: (1) The precious metals are the all-important measure of the wealth of a nation. (2) Aside from mining of ore, trade is the chief means of accumulating these precious metals in the shape of specie. (3) In order that this trade may be profitable, and specie accumulated, there must be a favorable balance of exports over imports. (4) To furnish markets for these exports and thus to create a favorable balance of trade for the mother country, colonies are valuable, if not indispensable. (5) In order that the colonies may furnish markets for finished products and a source of supply of raw materials, manufacturing must be forbidden in the colonies, lest they supply their own necessities and exhaust their stock of raw materials. (6) The colonies must thus be looked upon as primarily profitable commercial enterprises of the mother country.

We now know that this mercantilist argument was erroneous in many of its premises, particularly the notions that the supply of specie is the chief mark of national prosperity and that a favorable balance of trade necessarily means an increase in the domestic supply of available specie. We further know that these policies and practices greatly restricted the commercial activity and prosperity of the various European states. Inevitably, the sum of the small injuries inflicted by states on each other was detrimental to the European family of nations as a whole. These facts were not understood at the time, and this attitude of the state toward economic life persisted with little mitigation until the second quarter of the 19th century.

Along with the aspects and achievements of Mercantilism—which related to commercial and colonial policies and practices—went very important enactments in the way of the extension of state activity in economic affairs within the home boundaries. In England such things as the Statute of Apprentices introducing state control of labor and its conditions, the establishment of the price-fixing power of the justices of the peace, and the state control of industrial life by public proclamation are significant cases in point. In France, the state enforcement of guild practices and morés, the digging of canals, erection of public buildings, and the reclamation of land are achievements associated with Jean-Baptiste Colbert and his assistants and successors. Even more thoroughgoing was the state intervention in the field of national economic life and public finance in Prussia, which was guided by the German Mercantilists or Cameralists and most thoroughly executed under the aegis of Frederick the Great.

In Germany the mercantilist trend was known as Cameralism, and was colored by the peculiar circumstances which existed there as compared with the mercantile states like England, France and Spain. The problem of foreign trade being far less important at that date in Germanic states, the philosophy of extensive state intervention was naturally turned more toward domestic economic and political problems.

Statue of Adam Smith from the rear of the Royal Academy, London.

CHAPTER EIGHTEEN

Mercantilism Versus The Concept of National Identity

W hile the East India trade was one of the outstanding vehicles of opposition to mercantilist restrictions, underneath the actual propaganda flowed a deep stream of new economic and social thought, some of the sources of which were far from being of a purely business nature. Though the merchant classes, including Cromwell, their arch-representative in England for a decade, started out with a firm belief in Mercantilism, many changed their minds when they saw the relationship of the system to royal absolutism and taxation. As their interests broadened out beyond what they had at first anticipated, they saw their march to prosperity hampered at many points. In the same way that they had objected to arbitrary royal taxation and insisted upon the right of Parliament to decide these matters, so later many individuals and private groups came to chafe at state interference in general. As is quite common with human beings, they identified their own advantage with that of society. The pamphleteers for the most part did not base their attacks upon Mercantilism upon a direct and open statement of their interests, but sought for a general and social philosophy that should include the aspirations of their class. This philosophy they found ready-made in the deductions which had grown up with modern critical thought, founded especially upon the scientific progress of their own century.

Remarkable development in natural science, from Nicolaus Copernicus to Isaac Newton especially, had suggested that nature manifests itself according to certain immutable laws. In particular, this notion had been derived from the celestial mechanics of Newton, with his formulation of the law of universal gravitation. The new natural science had been seized upon by a group of writers interested in philosophy and theology, the so-called deists and rationalists. These thinkers held that society, in all its manifestations and institutions, no less than physical nature itself, is subject to the reign of natural law. Natural law was assimilated to, and regarded as identical with, divine law. Thus it was assumed that the laws of nature were an expression of the divine will and, therefore, benign in their operations. From this they reasoned that man should endeavor to allow the natural order of things to govern his social, political and economic life. This would be brought about more certainly than in any other way, they thought, by allowing free and unlimited competition and individualism to dominate all phases of economic policy and activity.

All this implied, when it did not especially urge, that the states should refrain from all activity in the economic field beyond the minimum of interference necessary to secure protection of life and property and the enforcement of contracts; that all public regulation of economic activities should cease; and that a regime of individualism, competition and free trade should be instituted. The doctrine, with its implications, was first thoroughly formulated by a group of French writers known as the physiocrats.

The physiocratic theories were taken up and elaborated by a remarkable group of English economic writers. Adam Smith, whose *Wealth of Nations* appeared in print in 1776, was the first and most famous. There was one notable difference in the English interpretation. The physiocrats had represented mining and agriculture as the sole productive industries, but the English writers adapted their doctrines to the new economic tendencies of the time and laid special stress upon manufacturing and commerce as the chief sources of income in national wealth. These men, even Adam Smith, were already standing on the threshold of a new era of individualism, and their illustrations of older economic theories give these a vitality and reality to us which they do not possess in their original form. The economic thought of Smith, Malthus, Ricardo, and the two Mills, among others, varies so much from their French predecessors that they are usually distinguished from the physiocrats by the term "classical economists."

Some slight effects of these attempts to apply the idea of natural law and natural liberty to economics were visible at the outset. Turgot, the contemporary and friend of Adam Smith, attempted to reform French finances in 1774, and was willing to go to great lengths if the opportunity offered, but his initial measures proved unwelcome to the privileged classes and he was driven from office. English parliamentary debates show the influence of the *Wealth of Nations* up to the French Revolution, the excesses of which gave a temporary check to the whole notion of natural liberty. It was not until well along in the 19th century that serious attempts were made to realize free trade, in France, Germany and England.

A photograph of a selection of Delftware.

CHAPTER NINETEEN

The Stimulation
Of Manufacturing

O ne of the most important indirect results of the Commercial Revolution was its stimulation of European manufacturing, particularly in England. The new overseas markets called for vast quantities of European manufactured products, and the governments stressed those to be exchanged for raw materials. No doubt the flow of goods was checked somewhat by monopoly and Mercantilism, but it was unprecedented, nevertheless.

The textile industry was one of the first to be profoundly affected by the new demand. The manufacture of woolens had been highly developed in Flanders in the Middle Ages and had been introduced into England after the middle of the 14th century. The silk industry had also grown to some proportions in Italy and France and, to a lesser degree, in England. There was relatively little cotton manufacturing carried on in Europe until the opening of the 18th century, though some cotton cloth is known to have been produced in England as early as the 16th century.

Some of the overseas demand for European textiles came from natives, but far more of it from colonists. Among the old, established industries to profit by the new situation were English woolens and French silks. The fact that some of this trade was with tropical or subtropical regions led to a remarkable development of the cotton trade, in spite of the opposition of the vested interests in the woolen and silk industries. As early as the latter half of the 16th century the English began a coarse cloth known as fustian for export to the Indies. At the outset it was probably not cotton, certainly not all cotton, but it soon appears as a mixture in which cotton figured more and more as the importation of raw cotton into England increased. There also developed a considerable cotton industry in the manufacturing of calico, chintz and underclothing, but the woolen interests effectively obstructed the triumph of the new rival for a long period. It came to dominate English textile industry only after the onset of the Industrial Revolution of the 18th century. The early development of English specialization upon a rough, staple, cotton cloth was of great importance in facilitating the introduction of textile machinery, the ancient traditions, craft skill and guild vestiges in the woolen industry offering a much greater resistance to technological changes. A revolution in dyestuffs also improved the quality as well as increased the possible quantity of English colored fabrics. The most important of the new vegetable dyes from overseas were indigo, logwood and cochineal.

European manufacturers were also notably stimulated through the adoption of a number of new commodities from the East, particularly pottery, many types of hardware, glass, furniture (particularly upholstered furniture), tapestry and silks. The wide use of pottery in Europe came largely from the contact of Europeans with China. During the Middle Ages dishes had been made of wood, pewter or brass. Now Europeans, while still importing some porcelain objects from China, began to manufacture imitations of these Chinese goods, and we have the beginnings of such well known products as the Dresden ware and Delft ware. Allied with the pottery industry was the manufacture of clay pipes, which began after 1600, when tobacco was introduced from North America.

The leather industry increased to a marked degree, particularly notable being the enormous demand for shoes on the part of the colonists. In the year 1658, no less than 24,000 pairs of shoes were sent to Virginia alone.

There was a large demand for various types of hardware in the colonies, particularly for muskets, hoes, nails, swords, various types of tools, lead, pewter and tinware. The development of the hardware industry in turn stimulated mining, particularly the mining of iron, lead and tin. Various types of glass products and glazed ware first appeared in Europe on a considerable scale from the 17th century onward.

During the Middle Ages there had been little use of glass, except for windows in dwellings of the rich and the notable development of stained glass for cathedral windows. The glass industry in the Orient had been important since the days of the ancient Egyptians, and European contact with the East led to the large scale introduction of glass and glazed products. For that matter, the great glass windows of the medieval Gothic cathedrals had been constructed after the crusading expeditions to the Levant began in 1096. Not only was the use of glass and glazing popularized by the Commercial Revolution for such uses as windows and dishes, but many specialized products appeared, such as spectacles, burning glasses, mirrors and new devices brought forth as a result of the progress in the science of optics.

European taste in furniture also underwent a revolution as a result of contact with outside peoples. Most medieval furniture was crudely made and rarely upholstered. A desire for the sumptuous, comfortable and richly upholstered articles now grew up as a result of voyages to the East. New and admirable types of wood for such purposes came in from overseas, such as mahogany, rosewood and cedar. Gum varnishes of similar origin were utilized to give the new furniture a high polish and an attractive finish. European contact with the Japanese art of lacquering influenced these new developments to no inconsiderable degree. Not only was the furniture industry developed, but the new tastes were applied to such things as wainscoting, stairways etc, which were made of the newly imported woods and finished with the new varnishes.

Floors in the medieval period were usually bare or, at best, covered by reed or straw mats, but the use of carpets and rugs was now learned from the Orient. These, along with the new furniture and finishes, served to bring new standards of taste and comfort into European households. The wealthy continued as they have up to the present time, to import rugs and carpets from the Orient, but there soon developed a profitable industry in the manufacturing of these products in Europe.

Silks and tapestries had been imported into Europe from the East for a long time, and a considerable development had already taken place in the native European silk industry. This beginning was vastly stimulated by direct contact with the East. The quantity of silk clothing and tapestries demanded was much greater, while design and workmanship underwent a veritable revolution.

Ship-building was immediately and enormously affected by the new commerce. We have already seen how the change in the construction of vessels had been one of the most important influences making possible overseas expansion. Gradually but surely the ships were made more adaptable to the necessities and demands of oceanic navigation, and the progress in physics and mathematics made it possible to apply scientific rules to their construction. Improvements in the technique of ship-building tended to keep pace with the demand for more and better vessels.

The expansion of English shipping is characteristic. In 1560 the total tonnage of English merchant ships was 7,600. In 1691 it had increased to 500,000. This was paralleled by a remarkable growth in the tonnage of war vessels. The English naval tonnage in 1607 was 23,000 while a century later it reached over 120,000.

In addition to these major phases of industrial change resulting from the Commercial Revolution, there are others of minor though significant proportions. One of these was the manufacture of trinkets for trade with the natives. While this never promised to become a great, permanent national industry, it did furnish work for large numbers of individuals during the 16th, 17th and 18th centuries, and was the basis of defrauding the natives on a huge scale. The introduction of precious metals and stones in larger quantities, and the opportunity for copying foreign work, led to a great development of the jewelry industry. The manufacture of new scientific instruments for navigation, such as the quadrant, sextant, chronometer, reflectors and telescopes, was practically a new craft. Pictures were produced for market on a considerable scale for the first time. Gunpowder-making occupied a more important place than we can easily realize, the muskets being used for hunting as well as for warfare, and there were so many frontiers! Enormous quantities of salt had to be mined or separated, since it was the one known preservative of fish and meat at sea.

"One of the most important indirect results of the Commercial Revolution was its stimulation of European manufacturing, particularly in England. The new overseas markets called for vast quantities of European manufactured products, and the governments stressed those to be exchanged for raw materials."

Photograph of factory workers winding large rotating and stationary armatures.

CHAPTER TWENTY

Preparation for the Industrial Revolution

The various commercial, financial and industrial results of the Commercial Revolution had their most important influence upon European society in preparing the way for the great Industrial Revolution which was to transform completely the culture of the western world in the century and a half following 1750. The new commerce created a large supply of available capital. It hastened the growth of capitalism, credit and credit institutions. It trained and encouraged Europe in the way of investments, speculation, and business enterprise. It greatly stimulated European manufacturing industry, tended to weaken the old restrictive guild system (even producing a preliminary type of factory system), and developed a larger and more highly specialized industrial population. In these and various other ways the Commercial Revolution prepared the way for the Industrial Revolution.

There has been for a long time a good-natured controversy between certain economic and social historians as to whether the Commercial or the Industrial Revolution was the more important influence in modern times. This controversy is essentially futile as it implies a decision as to whether cause or effect is more influential in history. For practical purposes, it may be held that while the Industrial Revolution has created far more sweeping changes in European society than its predecessor, these later transformations would have been impossible without the profound alterations in European society produced by the Commercial Revolution.

Thomas Weaver's painting of agriculturalist Thomas Coke, 1st Earl of Leicester (1754-1842).

CHAPTER TWENTY-ONE

The Agricultural Revolution

long with the development of manufacturing as a result of the Commercial Revolution went the stimulation of other forms of industry, such as fishing and agriculture. For centuries the fisheries constituted an important element in the industrial and commercial life of Europe. They were greatly increased in scope and form by the growth of overseas trade and contacts. Not only was the amount of fishing carried on in the European waters notably affected, in order to supply the increased demand of the continent itself, but new areas were opened to exploitation, particularly along the coast of North America. New markets for the products of the fisheries were discovered in the tropical and semi-tropical colonies, especially in the West Indies, which consumed great quantities of salt fish. In addition to the salt fish itself, other important commodities, such as oil and whalebone, were provided through the fisheries. The greatly increased use of salt fish also stimulated the development of the salt industry.

Even more revolutionary were the changes in agriculture between 1600 and 1800, most notably in England. The English developments are more significant from the standpoint of the general economic history of Europe because of their closer relationship with the Industrial Revolution.

While the connection between the new commerce and the greatly stimulated manufacturing industry, on the one hand, and the expansion of Europe, on the other, is clear and obvious enough, it may not appear so evident that the Agricultural Revolution, which we are about to describe, was directly related to the results of the overseas expansion. A little reflection will, however, reveal the fundamental dependence of the agricultural transformation upon the preceding developments in commerce and industry. A number of the new agricultural products came from extra-European areas. The capital, which did more than anything else to break up the medieval manorial system, was accumulated chiefly as a result of the new commercial activity. It was the modern commercial activity which produced the merchant princes who wished to secure social and political prestige through purchasing great landed estates and thus establishing themselves in the grand manner essential to social success in the England of that day. Finally, it was the capital which they had acquired through commercial pursuits which enabled Thomas Coke and others like him to carry on capitalistic farming on a large scale. The Agricultural Revolution, then, cannot be divorced from the general complex of economic, social and cultural changes which grew out of the expansion of Europe from the days of the Crusades onward.

The manorial system had been wiped out in England, as far as methods of land-holding and class differentiation were concerned, by the 15th century, but the technique of agriculture, with respect to tools and cooperative labor, underwent astonishingly slight changes between the 12th century and the 17th. But a series of remarkable changes in technique, with the resulting reaction upon the social organization of English agriculture, took place in the 18th century. They may be summarized under the general heading of the introduction of new implements, successful experiments with new crops, improvements of stock-breeding, drainage of waste land and development of scientific notions of fertilizing the soil and, finally, the organization of scientific and pseudo-scientific societies for the promotion of improved agricultural technique. All of these innovations were facilitated by the rise of modern capital which, for the first time, put at the disposal of agriculture a sufficient pecuniary backing to make possible the introduction of new and more advanced methods.

In France and Germany, as in England, the new trade stimulated by the Crusades and the impecuniosity of the feudal nobles led to a general decay of serfdom. This was checked in Germany, especially in eastern Germany, by the Thirty Years' War (1618-48), and serfdom actually increased. It must not be forgotten that the Commercial Revolution was well under way by this time, that capitalism was developing rapidly and hence that the growth of serfdom in eastern Germany was accompanied by the consolidation of estates considerably different from medieval manors. Junker farming had many quite modern aspects, in spite of its anachronistic labor system. In many respects the great estates were progressive as to methods of cultivation, with much enclosed land, well-bred stock and an increasing amount of grain raising for market. Western Germany—especially southwestern Germany—was more like France. During French Revolutionary and Napoleonic times it became a part of the French system for a time, and never quite relapsed into the old looseness of organization or shook off the influence of the Code Napoleon.

The decay of both manorialism and serfdom was more pronounced and continuous in France than in Germany for two main reasons, besides many lesser ones: France was more involved in the expansion of Europe and the Commercial Revolution, and her highly centralized national government encouraged the shift to a taxable money economy, at the same time that it sternly suppressed the feudal barons. By 1774 only about six percent of the population was in a state of even nominal serfdom, and her finance minister, Necker, correctly characterized rural France just before the Revolution as "an immensity of small rural properties."

When the Industrial Revolution began about the middle of the 18th century in England, she was not only more highly industrialized already than either France or Germany, but her agriculture had also been placed on a more thoroughly capitalistic basis. Her overseas colonies and stations gave her a great advantage in both raw materials and markets. The wars and blockades from 1792 to 1815 gave her a chance to consolidate an enduring industrial supremacy on the basis of these advantages already won. Both England and Germany had one potential superiority over France which was to become more and more apparent during the 19th century. Their population was far from the maximum which the soil could support, whereas this factor had largely stabilized and crystallized French society for centuries. Swift economic change was impossible in France for want of elbow room, but England had only to grow, dumping any surplus of goods and people in her empire outside. While Germany was to find imperial growth difficult for want of unpreempted waste spaces, her people were willing to emigrate, and an era of relatively free trade was to give her an opportunity for economic expansion partially compensating for her political limitations and backwardness.

Engraving of Peter the Great (1672-1725) from *Rambaud's Russia*, frontispiece, 1898.

CHAPTER TWENTY-TWO

The Rise of the Absolute Dynastic State

One of the most important of the political results of European expansion was the rise of the modern national and centralized states. It had been from necessity, not choice, that medieval kings had supported the feudal system, since they depended upon the lords for their royal revenue, for their soldiers and, to a very large extent, for the administration of justice. Nothing could be more natural than that the feudal barons should hesitate to render services or to make contributions to any individual or cause which looked forward to the reduction of their own power and prestige. As already pointed out, the feudal system was merely the best substitute which could be found for a more centralized government in an agricultural society without any great volume of trade or store of precious metals.

The various civil and religious wars of late medieval and early modern times did a great deal toward reducing the power of the feudal lords. Such tendencies were especially well illustrated by the English "Wars of the Roses" (1455-1487) and the French religious wars of the 16th century. But this self-destruction of the power of the lords was not sufficient; what was needed was a large independent source of income for the king. This was at last provided through the various benefits derived by the monarchs from overseas trade and colonization. They received some income from the discovery of precious metals, some from their share in public piracy or privateering, some from chartering commercial companies and the granting of monopolies, and some from custom duties on the increased foreign trade. In addition, there gradually grew up the practice of direct taxation. For the time being, this enabled the king to hire his officials and soldiers and begin the process of destroying the power of the feudal lords. In the long run, the middle class, through its parliaments, asserted the right to determine the nature and extent of this taxation.

In England, the feudal regime ended and a strong monarchy was established when Henry VII founded the Tudor line in 1485. In Spain the centralizing process was pretty well advanced by 1556. Henry IV of France established the strong Bourbon dynasty in 1589, and by 1652 all serious threats of political feudalism against the absolute monarch had practically disappeared. Russia, under Peter the Great (1689-1725), imitated France, and a little over a century after the establishment of the Bourbon dynasty, Peter had crushed local government and given relatively permanent centralization to the vast empire in eastern Europe and Asia. Working upon the foundation laid by the first elector in the last half of the previous century, Prussia had evolved a highly centralized kingdom by 1713. In this way the national state system emerged from the feudal order of the Middle Ages.

The rise of the fairly centralized national state in the place of the provincial and localized feudal entity was the chief political achievement of early modern times, but within the general framework of the national state there developed successively two widely different states of organization and control. In the first, the absolute power of the king was the outstanding fact; in the second this power was largely captured by parliaments.

While the rise of the individual ruler to power was the striking thing about these new states, as seen by contemporary observers, it was not their most permanent feature. The king was confused with the state, and often regarded himself as practically identical with it. Back of the visible clashes of kings with popes was the more general struggle between secular and religious authority which had gone on with varying fortunes throughout the Middle Ages; but the new national states were in a position to triumph completely. The "divine-right" theory of kings was taken right out of the Middle Ages. Here identical claims had been made by the Holy Roman emperors and the lawyer courtiers, like Pierre Dubois and Marsiglio of Padua, who supported them and various kings against papal encroachments. After the

12th century revival of the Roman law, which emphasized the supremacy of the state and the prince, the earlier advantages of the
church in the contest were steadily undermined. The notion of divine
kingship helped to capture for the national state the popular awe
which had attached itself to the semi-spiritual sway of church and empire. Machiavelli's *The Prince* laid great stress upon *Realpolitik* or
practical methods and also upon the supremacy of the monarch. Still
later, Thomas Hobbes vigorously defended secular absolutism. Besides
its sheer might and growing riches, the state gained respect and dig-
nity through the rise of modern commerce and colonies, which
greatly increased the range of problems which needed to be settled by
central civil authorities. It should be noted that the absolute state,
which brooks no opposition to its authority, is not necessarily associated with absolute monarchy, or with monarchy of any kind, as wit-
nessed by Soviet Russia or any of the republics in World War II.

American colonists pull down a statue of King George III, July 9, 1776.

CHAPTER TWENTY-THREE

The Bourgeoisie and Representative Government

The absolute monarchs owed their ascendancy in no small measure to the aid of the merchant and professional classes. These, remembering the depredations and persecutions of the feudal lords in the Middle Ages, joined enthusiastically with the aspiring kings to crush feudalism. In the period which followed they became the basis of the new system of administration. In due time, however, the merchant classes found that the new kings tended to threaten their interests and limit their independence quite as much as the feudal lords had done earlier. When the arbitrary royal power openly threatened the interests of the merchant classes, they tended to organize in opposition to the absolute monarchs and subject them to constitutional limitations.

From the English Revolution of 1644-1649 to the Russian Revolution of 1905, the most characteristic political development in European society was the uprising of the middle classes against the absolute monarchs and the resulting evolution of parliamentary and constitutional government. Early historians, such as Thomas Carlyle, Jules Michelet, and George Bancroft, looked upon such movements as the French and American revolutions as divinely guided epics, but we now know that these, along with the English revolutions of the 17th century, were but specific manifestations of the growth of the middle-class power.

The middle class developed a body of economic and political theory to justify its attitudes and programs. We have already seen that in the field of economic theory it gradually came to favor a complete withdrawal of the state from all types of interference with economic life. In the field of political theory the middle class developed a related type of interpretation. What it desired above all was freedom from arbitrary taxation and other forms of oppression. Hence it developed a doctrine of the natural rights of man to life, liberty and property. This theory of natural rights was closely allied to the natural order which lay at the foundation of the economic philosophy of *laissez-faire*. These natural rights of life, liberty, and property, which included the specific freedom from arbitrary imprisonment or taxation, were held by these writers to be inherent in the order of things from the beginnings of human society. The state or civil authority was established, not to limit or terminate these supposed inherent rights, but rather still more firmly to ensure and protect them.

Assaults upon absolutism were thus philosophically justified and the middle class worked out a theory of the right of revolution. It was held that originally men had lived in a state of nature, which became confused and inconvenient because of the rise of property and the consequent development of human selfishness. In order to assure peace and safety, it was necessary to create a superior authority—the state—to maintain order and to preserve the natural rights of each and all. A governing group, said the natural rights philosophers, was then chosen by the people, the new rulers agreeing to abide by certain general terms in the "compact" thus created. In case the rulers violated the terms of the original agreements, it was not only the right but the duty of the people to rise up and drive them from power, substituting new authorities who would agree to abide by the terms of the contract.

It was this type of theory which developed as an apologetic for the English revolutions of the 17th century and used as the justification for the American and French revolutions. By far the most influential writer of this group that stressed the importance of the social and governmental contracts was John Locke. Many of his theories were taken up and popularized in America and France by such writers as Thomas Jefferson and Jean Jacques Rousseau. It is somewhat astonishing to note the number of points of correspondence between this body of doctrine and that of the medieval theologians, from Archbishop Hincmar of Lyons in the 9th century to St.Thomas Aquinas in the 13th, his disciple Agidus Romanus,William of Occam and Marsiglio of Padua in the early 14th, and men like Jean Gerson and Nicholas of Cues in the 15th.

New illustrative material on the primitive peoples overseas now appeared, often false or misinterpreted, which seemed to many to vindicate the historic accuracy of the doctrine of an original state of nature, prior to organized society. There was no real historical foundation, however, for the beliefs about natural rights or early social contracts. Most of the assumptions about liberty and equality which are so familiar to us through the writings of Rousseau and Jefferson have been swept away by modern biological, psychological, anthropological and historical research. The vigor and success of "Rousseauism," as we might call it, had no apparent connection with the scientific truth or untruth of its doctrines. It is to be explained rather by the trends and interests of society which thus rationalized its interests and aspirations.

Sculpture of Alexander Hamilton in front of the U.S. Treasury Building in Washington.
Photo by Alex Wong. © Getty Images, ID: treasur22000_20010629_40508.jpg.

CHAPTER TWENTY-FOUR

The Significance of the English, French & American Revolutions

We cannot deal in any detail with these revolutions, but it seems worthwhile to indicate briefly the manner in which they exemplified the rise of the middle class. The English Revolution of 1645-1649, which was extended in its achievements by that of 1688-89, definitely ended absolute monarchy in England and established the supremacy of Parliament, the representative branch of the government. This was the essence of the middle-class political program. While the powerful landlord class was by no means completely subordinated at this time, English political and legal institutions were successfully adapted to the aspirations of the bourgeoisie. Under such ministers as Horace Walpole, English institutions were conducted primarily in the interest of growing trade and commerce, and the classes which profited thereby.

The American Revolution of 1775-83, which detached the 13 colonies of the Atlantic seaboard from the European system, was also primarily a revolt and triumph of the commercial classes. While as Professor Arthur Schlesinger has shown, the powerful merchant classes did not actually desire an open revolution, they had hoped to intimidate England into discontinuance of the new commercial policy which had been determined upon in 1763. Ultimately the movement they had initiated among the mobs of the coast towns grew into open rebellion, which they found themselves pledged to support. After independence had been achieved, however, the merchant class gave up most of the radical notions of the revolutionary period and framed a relatively conservative constitution designed to restore financial stability, promote commerce, and in other ways to advance the interests of the business classes. The leader of this group was Alexander Hamilton, perhaps the greatest economic statesman in American history. Even the Latin-American revolutions had a powerful economic foundation, in that they were encouraged by England, which stood to profit greatly by the increased freedom of trade.

The French Revolution was also clearly an example of the increased power of the bourgeoisie group. In the 17th century the middle class had attempted to secure a reform of the policies of the state, particularly the internal economic policies—but the dynasty and the landlords were too strong. By the close of the 18th century the middle class had become powerful enough to defy the monarchy and successfully attack the economic and social vestiges of French feudalism. France was reorganized in line with the programs and practices of the middle class—a tendency carried still further by Napoleon, who based his system primarily upon the notion of the placation, and in some cases the elevation, of the bourgeoisie.

It should be kept in mind that these achievements in the way of establishing parliamentary ascendancy over absolute monarchy lacked any marked tendency toward the genuinely popular government which we call democracy. They were rather a preparation for, than an actual realization of, democratic institutions. In no country could a majority of the people cast ballots for the election of representatives. Economic and political activities were still based upon the notion of privilege and position. Not until the 19th century, with the growth of the industrial proletariat and of the frontier element in the United States, was there any conspicuous success in the way of actual democracy.

"It should be kept in mind that these achievements in the way of establishing parliamentary ascendancy over absolute monarchy lacked any marked tendency toward the genuinely popular government which we call democracy. They were rather a preparation for, than an actual realization of, democratic institutions."

Illustration of John Locke.

CHAPTER TWENTY-FIVE

Legal Developments

The legal changes of this age paralleled the social and political evolution. Feudal law was gradually replaced by national codes, comprehensive in scope and savage in nature, which penalized with special severity any acts which challenged royal supremacy. When the middle class gradually came into greater political power, they were particularly interested in protecting property and business enterprises from arbitrary royal interference and confiscation. Hence, the chief influence of the bourgeoisie upon jurisprudence was to emphasize the function of the state in protecting private property, and to stress the desirability of non-interference on the part of state in business activities. John Locke, perhaps the most influential political writer of the age, openly contended that the chief purpose of the state was the protection of property. The natural right doctrine was invoked and elaborated to support these basic dogmas of the sanctity of property and freedom of business.

It was here, then, that there originated that type of juristic thought and practice which has served as the bulwark of the protection of business against social regulation, and has found its finest flower in the "due process" clause of the Fourteenth Amendment to the federal Constitution of the United States. At the close of the 18th century and throughout the 19th there developed that great movement for constitutions which were designed to give property not only the protection of statutory law, but also that much more profound and impregnable type of privilege involved in the immunities of constitutional provisions and constitutional law.

Dublin Castle was once the seat of British colonial administration in Ireland and the repository of the Irish crown jewels until their theft in 1907. It was formally handed over to the administration of the of the new Irish Republic in December 1921 with the signing of the Anglo-Irish treaty, ending British rule in Ireland.

CHAPTER TWENTY-SIX

Origins of Modern Colonial Administration

One of the most important phases of political and legal development connected with the expansion of Europe was the rise of new methods of colonial administration. The Persians and Romans had faced the problems of colonial control, but the acquisition of colonies overseas raised new issues and promoted the development of modern methods of colonial rule. In general, European colonial rule to 1800 was characterized by the subordination of colonies to the mother country, by extensive administrative interference of the mother country in colonial politics, by slight prevalence of local self-government, by extensive land grants to individuals, by forced labor by natives, and by the domination of monopoly and special economic privileges.

The degree to which self-government was encouraged differed greatly as between the British and non-British colonies. England alone made any important concessions to the self-governing principle. Starting out with three types of colonies—provincial, corporate and proprietary—England tried to reduce her American colonies, as far as possible, to the royal provincial type. As a result, there developed a struggle between the interference of the mother country through the royal governor and the principle of self-government as represented in the elective branch of the colonial legislatures. This popular element in the colonial legislatures provided one of the chief sources for training in the principles of representative government during the 18th century. The English alone permitted sufficient colonial autonomy to make possible the rise of what was really a new society in the western world at this time.

We have already seen, in discussing the mercantilistic system, that the mother countries used their political systems as the basis for elaborate control of the economic life of her colonies. The British commercial policies and administration were far more liberal than those of other states, but even the British methods served to promote revolt on the part of the colonies. This revolt was a leading cause of that modification of British colonial policy which furnished the model for 19th century developments in liberalized colonial administration.

SELECTED REFERENCES:

I.

Abbott, W. C., *The Expansion of Europe;* Ballard, C. A., *America and the Atlantic;* Beazley, C. R., *Henry the Navigator;* Bolton, H. E. and Marshall, T. M., *The Colonization of North America;* Bourne, E. G., *Spain in America;* Cheyney, E. P., *The European Background of American History;* Cunningham, W., *Western Civilization in Its Economic Aspects,* Vol. II; Day, C., *A History of Commerce;* Gibbons, H. D. B., *A History of Commerce;* Gillespie, J. E., *A History of Europe, 1500-1815;* Jacobs, J., *The Story of Geographical Discovery;* Jayne, K. G., *Vasco da Gama and His Successors;* Keller, A. G., *Colonization;* Morris, H. C., *History of Colonization;* Moses, B., *Spain Overseas;* Muir, Ramsey, *The Expansion of Europe;* Thwaites, R. G., *France in America;* Tyler, L. G., *England in America.*

II.

Ashley, W. J., *The Economic Organization of England;* Botsford, J. B., *English Society in 18th century;* Corti, Count, *The Rise of the House of Rothschild;* Cunningham, W., *Western Civilization in Its Economic Aspects,* Vol. II.; Day, C., *A History of Commerce;* Gide, C., and Rist, C., *A History of Economic Doctrines;* Ehrenberg, R., *Capital and Finance in the Age of the Renaissance: A Study of the Fuggers;* Gillespie, J. E., *The Influence of Overseas Expansion on England to 1700;* Higgs, H., *The Physiocrats;* Hobson, J. A., *The Evolution of Modern Capitalism;* Horrocks, J. W., *A Short History of Mercantilism;* Knight, M. M., Barnes, H. E., and Flugel, F., *Economic History of Europe;* Prothero, R. E., *English Farming, Past and Present;* Renard, G., and Weulersse, G., *Life and Work in Modern Europe;* Schapiro, J. S., *Social Reform and the Reformation;* See, Henri, *Economic and Social Conditions in France During the 18th century; The Origins of Modern Capitalism;* Shepherd, W. R., "The Expansion of Europe" in *Political Science Quarterly,* 1919; Smith, P., *The Age of the Reformation;* Sombart, W., *The Quintessence of Capitalism;* Unwin, G., *Industrial Organization in the Sixteenth and Seventeenth Centuries;* Usher, A. P., *An Introduction to the Industrial History of England;* Weber, M., *General Economic History.*

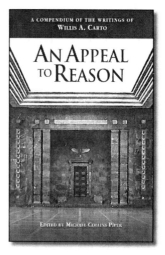

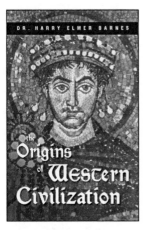

MONEY

THE 12TH & FINAL RELIGION

Money? A Religion?
And Just 12 Religions?
What Does it All Mean?

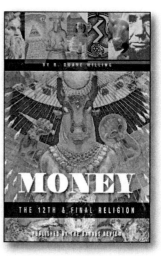

AUTHOR R. DUANE WILLING gives you the key to understanding why the illuminated ones of the New World Order need to substitute secrecy for justice. Learn how God Moloch, devoid of any capacity for either mercy or forgiveness, is moving with brute force for world control behind the myth called Israel. The Moloch conceals the invention of credit based money. Belief in money drives the human condition to prey on the planet and its inhabitants. Money creation has Biblical consequences called usury. The key to usury is hidden in the legend of the Holy Grail. The covenant obligation to take dominion and prosper in harmony with nature is subverted by secretive organizations. There is talk of Bilderbergers and various councils and globalist corporations. As if by design, the collective mind remains hypnotized by their Moloch magic of central banking with its perpetual (National) debts, money at interest and stock exchanges and income taxes.

For R. Duane Willing web site and blog enter: "The 12th and Final Religion" in your search engine.

More copies can be purchased from THE BARNES REVIEW history magazine at $17 each plus $3 S&H. For more than five copies call the publisher at 202-547-5586. Send payment to TBR, P.O. Box 15877, Washington, D.C. 20003. See more at www.barnesreview.org.

U.S. FINANCIAL PREDICAMENT PREDICTED BY MALAYSIAN MATTHIAS CHANG; NOW THE PREDICTIONS ARE COMING TRUE . . .

FUTURE FASTFORWARD:
THE ZIONIST ANGLO-AMERICAN EMPIRE MELTDOWN

Is global "Empire Capitalism" about to come crashing down? Will there be a worldwide "people's war" against the super-capitalists and their Zionist allies? Is nuclear war inevitable? Is the alliance between the United States, the British Empire, and Israel a paper tiger or a mighty empire? These are just some of the provocative questions addressed in *Future FastForward*, a forthright, no-holds-barred book by globe-trotting diplomat Matthias Chang, top-level political secretary for Malaysia's Mahathir Mohammad. **Softcover, 400 pages, #444, $25.**

BRAINWASHED FOR WAR:
PROGRAMMED TO KILL

In *Brainwashed for War: Programmed to Kill*, written by internationally renowned Malaysian barrister Matthias Chang, we learn that we Americans have been brainwashed for war our entire lives. From the Cold War of our youths to Vietnam and now the so-called "War Against Terror" we have been lied to, mind-controlled and duped by leader after leader with the goal of making us mindless supporters of bloody war. Tracing back four decades and more, *Brainwashed for War* documents the atrocities carried out by the imperialist, Zionist-driven forces whose goal it is to subjugate the peoples of the world. **Softcover, 556 pages, #460, $30.**

SPECIAL: Both books for just $50.

Add $3 S&H per book or $5 S&H per combo set inside the U.S. Outside the U.S. email tbrca@aol.com for S&H rates to your nation. To order send payment using the form on page 64 to TBR, P.O. Box 15877, Washington, D.C. 20003 or call **1-877-773-9077** toll free to charge to Visa or MasterCard.

No Beauty in the Beast:
Israel Without Her Mascara

Christ rejected their supremacist agenda and was crucified. Today we must recognize the supremacist ideology of Zionism for what it really is: The 'Beast' of St. John's Revelation!

NO BEAUTY IN THE BEAST: ISRAEL WITHOUT HER MASCARA is a book that discusses the most momentous events of mankind's history and how they pertain to today. What the world is witnessing today, with regard to the events in the Middle East and the manner in which the Christian West has been seduced into involving itself in the slaughter of innocent people, is the extension of the same battle that took place in the Palestinian town of Jerusalem 2,000 years ago between Jesus and the founders of the modern-day ideological movement of Zionism. Today, this Beast of Judeo-ethnocentrism against which Christ waged his war of liberation—the Beast which for 1,900 years remained dormant—has now been resurrected from the ashes where it remained safely isolated from the rest of mankind. It is at present devouring everything in its path to world domination. With the recreation of the state of Israel that was destroyed some 2,000 years ago and the much prophesied "return of the Jews" to the Holy Land, the world is now witnessing the fulfillment of the prophecies concerning a massive battle between the forces of good and evil. The ascendancy of Zionism—this same supremacist agenda that was opposed by Christ—is the linchpin to understanding the cryptic description of the Beast of the Apocalypse. And, just as was predicted by seers thousands of years ago, the future of humanity hangs in the balance. Written by TBR contributing board member Mark Glenn.

Softcover, 320 pages, #470, $25

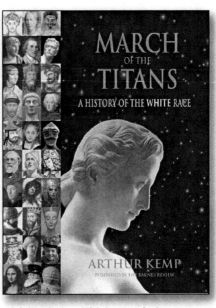

Auschwitz:
The Final Count

AUSCHWITZ: The very name of the infamous concentration camp in Poland has become synonymous with the period now commonly referred to as "the holocaust."

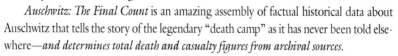

For about 60 years, schoolchildren around the world have been taught that 4 million Jews were exterminated in the gas chambers at Auschwitz. In other words, *Auschwitz alone accounts for 2/3 of the symbolic 6 million figure.*

But lo and behold: Even the Auschwitz authorities admit the 4 million figure is in need of "revision," lowering the total recently from 4 million to 1.5 million deaths at the camp.

But just how low can we go?

"An anthology of powerful history that blows apart one of the cornerstones of the Holocaust legend." —Willis A. Carto

Auschwitz: The Final Count is an amazing assembly of factual historical data about Auschwitz that tells the story of the legendary "death camp" as it has never been told elsewhere—*and determines total death and casualty figures from archival sources.*

This special anthology, featuring commentary by veteran British historian Vivian Bird (right), who originally edited this volume, offers an inside look at Auschwitz and provides the reader with scholarly information that had otherwise been unavailable or previously suppressed before publication of this book.

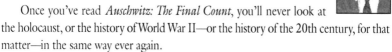

Once you've read *Auschwitz: The Final Count*, you'll never look at the holocaust, or the history of World War II—or the history of the 20th century, for that matter—in the same way ever again.

Softcover, 109 pages, #67, $13

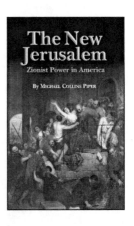

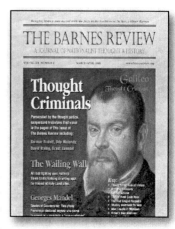

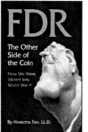

TBR ORDERING COUPON TBR subscribers take 10% off book prices

Item#	Description/Title	Qty	Cost Ea.	Total
	SUBTOTAL			
	Add S&H on books*			
Send a 1-year subscription to TBR for $46 plus my free book**				
Send a 2-year subscription to TBR for $78 plus two free books**				
	TOTAL			

*S&H ON BOOKS: Add $3 S&H for one item. Otherwise add $5 S&H on orders up to $50. Add $10 S&H on orders from $50.01 to $100. Add $15 S&H on orders over $100. Email tbrca@aol.com outside the U.S. for best S&H to your nation.

**OUTSIDE THE U.S: $65 for Canada/Mexico; $80 all others 1-year subscription via air mail.

PAYMENT OPTIONS: ❏ CHECK/MO ❏ VISA ❏ MASTERCARD

Card # _____

Expiration Date _____ Signature _____

OWC88

CUSTOMER INFORMATION:

NAME _____

ADDRESS _____

CIty/STATE/ZIP _____

RETURN WITH PAYMENT TO: THE BARNES REVIEW, P.O. Box 15877, Washington, D.C. 20003. Call 1-877-773-9077 toll free to charge to Visa or MasterCard. Outside U.S. emil TBRca@aol.com for book S&H to your nation.

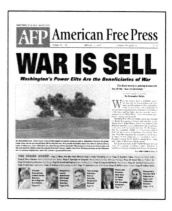